To the Reader,

Thank you for being interested in Adam's story. I hope you like it.

David Weaver

ONLY MORTALS CAN BE HEROES

A True Story
About Drug Addiction

by

David J. Weaver

Only Mortals Can Be Heroes
Copyright © 2005 by David J. Weaver
Special Premier Edition
ISBN 0-9770916-0-0
Library of Congress EPCN application in process.

Printed in the United States of America.

Edited by Daniel Lee Weaver
Jacket design by Barbara Glass Orris
Dust cover photo by Cover Studio, Johnstown, PA
Layout by Valley Printing Co., Johnstown, PA
Published by Cambria Creations, LLC
515 Main Street
Johnstown, PA 15901

ORDERING:
www.onlymortalscanbeheroes.com
1-(866)-246-1181
Or
www.atlasbooks.com
1-(800)-247-6553

TABLE OF CONTENTS

Foreword by D. Gerard Long, President Judge

Afterword by Raymond F. Dalton, Jr., Psychologist

AUTHOR'S NOTE

This story is told in the first person by Adam, the protagonist. But I wrote it. I am Adam's father. Although the words come out of Adam's mouth, he uses my pen.

All the events are supported by documents, such as medical records, police reports, photographs, court records, and the like. Some situations were not recorded contemporaneously with their occurrence. In these instances, accuracy was ensured with reference to Adam's notebook, an account he wrote as part of his therapy while undergoing drug rehabilitation. Although I am not the addict, let there be no mistaking that I lived through the episodes right along with Adam. Therefore, much of the story comes from my first-hand experience.

Every attempt was made to achieve authenticity. However, a few of the characters' names and identities were disguised to avoid embarrassment to them and possible recrimination against Adam.

David J. Weaver
Johnstown, Pennsylvania

The Problem

Being from a small town in Pennsylvania in the 50's, I was not exposed to drugs until I went to college. They had absolutely no appeal to me because I believed they were dangerous and would weaken a person's intellectual capacity. During the 60's while in college and law school in larger cities, I was certainly aware of drugs being used by others. In the last 30 years while I was a practicing attorney, a District Attorney, and a Judge, I have dealt with this problem on a daily basis.

Drugs are the cause, either directly or indirectly, of approximately 80 to 85 percent of all crimes committed. People are either buying or selling drugs, breaking into homes or pharmacies to get money for drugs, or shooting each other over the selling rights of drugs. All of which create a gigantic criminal caseload and many social problems.

It is evident that when a person is addicted to heroin, cocaine, Oxycontin, or other type of serious drug, there is a very low recovery rate. Thus, the outlook for an addict is extremely bleak. The life of someone addicted to one of these serious drugs is usually short term. It is a life full of misery and pain, for not only the addicts, but also their families and friends. Therefore, drugs are a scourge upon the citizens of our community and on the entire nation.

Our research has indicated that children in our community get exposed to drugs between the ages of 11 and 14. The Federal Government advises us to have preventative programs with students in fourth, fifth, and sixth grades. It is apparent that this is a problem affecting our youth at the most vulnerable time.

After questioning thousands of young people as to why they experimented with drugs, I have found that there are a variety of reasons. The overwhelming majority indicate that they just wanted to fit in with the crowd. A group of people they wish to be associated with were using drugs and they felt that this was the way to be accepted. The young usually start out with alcohol or marijuana, then go on to cocaine, Oxycontin, heroin, or methamphetamine. Many of these addicts appear before me crying in misery, along with disheartened parents and family. They indicate that it is a hopeless situation, after having tried therapy and finding it unsuccessful.

At present, we try to warn young children of the dangers of drugs by going into their schools when they are in fifth or sixth grade and having programs in the summer on the playgrounds to spread the message. It is quite clear that young people at this age do not want to listen to anybody over the age of 24. The young people feel that older speakers are completely out of touch with what the "in crowd" is doing. Therefore, we have people between the ages of 18 and 24 who are addicted and trying to help themselves, share their experiences with these young people.

Recognizing this drug problem, we now use a three-prong attack. First, we believe that responsible people have to educate against the dangers of drugs and its addiction. Second, we have to treat addicts who wish to be treated. And third, those who violate the law by ensnaring other people into this addiction must be punished.

Our treatment experience has shown us that the longer the treatment, the more chance of success. Two to four week therapy and education programs rarely prove to be successful. A program that lasts for 13 to 18 months is the major rehabilitation tool that we currently use. It is a waste of time, money, and effort to put someone into therapy who does not want to be in therapy or does not want to stop using drugs. Here again, the problem of what appeals to the youth is very important. When the use of drugs is glamorized in our culture, then it becomes more challenging for our educational programs about the dangers of drugs to be successful.

We have been in the middle of this problem since the 60's. The major impediments to ending it are: first, the high profit gained by selling drugs; second, the reluctance of youth to acknowledge the dangers of drugs; and third, the low rate of successful treatment for drug addicts. At present, we feel our three-prong program is the best course of action. But as long as the above three impediments are in place, it is going to be arduous to win this war. We realize that this is a very difficult situation, but we are confident that our efforts are proceeding in the right direction. We must continue to try to prevent drug usage because capitulation would be a disaster.

D. Gerard Long
President Judge
Court of Common Pleas
Cambria County, Pennsylvania

C H A P T E R   O N E

Busted

Being behind bars wasn't new to me. Six months earlier I got arrested for drug possession and spent one night in the Allegheny County jail in Pittsburgh. This time I was locked up in a holding cell at neighboring Westmoreland County Prison, sitting on a hardwood bench in handcuffs and leg irons. It was Christmas Eve 2002, and my head was starting to throb. It had been almost two days since my last fix.

Christmas Eve is supposed to be a holy night, but to me Christmas meant nothing. Most people think of Christmas as a time to spend with family and friends, a time to reflect on the blessings of life and to make plans for the upcoming year. I had no such thoughts. My mind was blank and my heart empty, without joy or spirit.

Although I hated being in jail, I made up my mind to take it like a man. I wasn't expecting anybody here to make excuses for my choices. I wasn't looking for anybody to believe my next lie, and I didn't expect anybody to care if my head throbbed. Look what ten years of doping got me! My 5' 11" body weighed a mere 120 pounds. Over that frail frame,

I draped a double "XX" shirt and hung baggy pants that barely stayed up. In a month, I would turn 21 in jail.

Leg irons held me fastened to a silver chain that ran through a three-inch iron ring that was bolted to the concrete floor. My hands were secured in the front by steel cuffs that seemed a little too tight on my wrist bones and looped through a leather belt designed to buckle behind my back. After a 40-minute wait, an armed constable slipped the chain out of my leg irons and allowed me to shuffle over to a bank of phones to place my call.

Mom and Dad had been divorced for over ten years. Which of my parents should I call? No sense calling Dad. He would not post money to get me out. Right now Mom was my best hope of making bail. Over Dad's objections, she was the one who bailed me out of the Allegheny County Jail six months ago.

The call went through collect, and Mom answered. Our conversation was brief. Mom flat out turned me down, saying not another penny should be wasted on me. Out of options, I had no choice but to wait in jail until sentencing.

My dad is a criminal defense lawyer. He was angry at me now. Still, I knew I could count on him for help after he calmed down. In the meantime, I was searching my brain to figure out how I could explain away 14 packets of heroin, a spoon, two syringes, and a small amount of marijuana. On second thought, why should I even try. It looked like I was going to be in jail for a while.

Just yesterday, I was living with my dad and my brother

2

Ben, who was home from college. Dad was taking his girlfriend Lisa to hear the Pittsburgh Symphony perform a Christmas special. He told me not to expect him home because he would be spending the night at the William Penn Hotel. The coast was clear after Dad and Lisa left for the concert.

My friend Eric and I also planned driving the 75-mile distance to Pittsburgh, but we had other reasons for making the trip. Female company was always desirable, so we called Cindy, knowing that she never refused a drug run. Everybody brought something to these get-togethers–gas, grass, or ass– and it didn't matter to Eric or me what Cindy would bring. As it worked out, Cindy supplied the weed, Eric drove his car, and I brought cocaine and heroin.

We started our trip by passing around a small roach which Cindy pulled from her purse. Forty-five minutes into our run, we had smoked two joints and had just finished burning our first rock. I had a syringe and heroin ready to mix, but that was for later. That is usually how it went. We would start out with something smooth and easy, like pot, and then progress to whatever stronger stuff we might have. Heroin was my favorite, but I'd use anything at all. When you're an addict, it doesn't matter what the dope is, you use it.

Since I was in the backseat, I really wasn't paying much attention to Eric's erratic driving. Apparently, a motorist following us down Route 22 observed suspicious activity in our car and reported it to the Pennsylvania State Police. A BOLO went out from Indiana County dispatch, and before any of us knew it, our Chevrolet Blazer was being closely followed by the Murrysville Police Department cruiser. Within a quarter of a mile, the cruiser activated its blue and red wigwags, forcing Eric to pull off the highway.

I had only a high school education, but I was street-smart. Experience told me the cop would search the vehicle for drugs after he stopped us, and I was certain he would do a pat down search on me as well. Being caught holding meant conviction, so I fumbled with my red ski jacket trying to empty the pockets before the officer reached the car door. If I could get the shit onto the floor somehow, the police would have a hard time proving whose it was–mine or Cindy's or Eric's.

I liked my chances, especially since it was Eric's car. Over the years, I learned bits and pieces of the law from my dad, and I knew that in order to be convicted of the crime of possession, the police had to find the dope on my person, not on the floor. Before the officer got to the car, I was able to ditch the heroin and one syringe, but I got caught with another syringe in my right coat pocket. My eyes were glazed, my movements were clumsy and slow, the perfect combination to cause the officer to alert on me. We were busted!

All three of us were driven to the police station where we were placed in separate rooms. Eric and Cindy provided written statements to the police, laying out the whole deal to them. Both were weak. So I might have expected them to talk. Not me. I like to think of myself as a tough guy, someone who will go down with his mouth shut. To me a snitch is the worst form of a lowlife. I have character.

After I learned the other two had ratted me out, I decided to come clean, hoping the cop would take it easy on me if I told the truth. Which I never did. Thinking quickly, I told the cop my dad was a lawyer, an officer of the court. I was pleading for a professional courtesy, one step removed. I gave the officer my dad's cell phone number, and, after the officer placed the call, I listened to his side of the conversation:

"Mr. Weaver, this is Officer Schellhammer with the Murrysville Police Department. We have your son Adam for possession of paraphernalia and possession of controlled substances. We'd like you to come get him."

(Pause)

"Looks like some marijuana and heroin."

(Pause)

"Yes sir, heroin."

(Pause)

"Ok sir, that's where he'll go then."

(Pause)

"Yes sir. Thank you, sir. Have a good evening."

Expectantly, I waited for the officer to explain the pick up arrangements. Instead, he turned to me and said, "Your dad thinks you need to go to jail, Adam, and that's where you're going."

As I was being cuffed and led to the police car for transport to the Westmoreland County Jail, I heard Cindy use the phone at the police station calling home for a ride for her and Eric. I thought to myself, "This is bullshit! My hotshot lawyer father lets me go to jail while the two snitches are going home."

I sat on the hardwood bench in the holding cell, listening to electronic clicks which activated the door separating me from 400 prisoners. Anxiously, I watched the door open and close, waiting for my turn to pass through. The high wore off hours ago, my head was hurting, and that heavy door kept opening and closing.

The day shift finished processing my paperwork and moved me to my assigned cell in general population. Hour by hour, I felt worse. I wanted to lie down and rest, but I was forced to leave the cell and join the herd for breakfast. I followed in line to the cafeteria where the rotted smell of whatever was cooking made me feel queasy. Aimlessly, I pushed my tray along the food line. By the time I reached the end, I was staring down at two mounds of mush and one puddle of yellow goop. I walked directly to the slop bucket and cleared my tray. For 20 minutes I sat shaking at the table until the mess hall emptied, at which time I made my way back to my block.

Finding my cell was confusing at first, because they all looked the same, and there were no physical features which might clue me on which was mine. The steel door to my cell had been stamped "G-37" right above the key hole. I remembered the number, so I went in. Restlessly I laid on my cot with an upset stomach trying to comprehend my predicament but not really making much sense of it. My head throbbed, signaling early-stage withdrawal.

At 11:30 a loud alarm sounded two short bursts throughout the prison, like a fire drill at school. It was chow time on the range, and once again I had no choice but to join the stampede. With effort, I managed to eat half of a grilled cheese sandwich, washing down each bite with coffee due to my inability to make saliva. The caffeine helped my head some, but not enough.

That evening the shakes hit, creating the odd sensation of being cold and hot at the same time. Sweat beaded everywhere on my body. My face flushed and my head pounded. Pacing the cell did not help nor did lying on the cot groaning. I wanted to let out a scream, but my cell mate, a burly white guy named Jordan, was already pissed off at me for invading his territory. I realized my incessant moans had taken him right to the edge, so I kept saying, "I'm sorry."

Jordan kept saying, "Shut the fuck up!"

The one place to vomit was the commode, but Jordan had that covered 24/7. I puked all over myself and the cot. Jordan jumped off the toilet and screamed that he was going to "fucking kill me." Helpless to defend, I covered up and waited for the blows. The way I felt at that time, death at the hands of my friend, Jordan, would have been an act of mercy toward me. When you go through withdrawal, you want to die. Anybody going through withdrawal wants to die. I don't care who you are.

That one day I spent in the Allegheny County jail six months earlier did not prepare me for the months of hard time that lay ahead. I didn't know what to expect. I thought, like a lot of people think, that life behind bars is a picnic. No bills to pay. Good food. Television. Free health care. Gymnasium facilities and a workout room. All of the fun things in life with none of the problems. My pap used to get worked up when he read in the newspaper about some criminal who was sentenced to prison. "That's too good a place for him. He'll have it made. Why should I bust my ass to pay taxes so that a useless son-of-a-bitch can have a good time in jail?" Pap was wrong. Nobody was having a good time here.

Jordan and I shared a toilet that sat against the back wall of our 8' x 12' space. The truth is we didn't share the toilet; it belonged to Jordan. I used it whenever I could. He used it whenever he wanted. The pot was a solid stainless steel fixture sitting in the open. Through the bars I could see six other commodes in six other 8' x 12' cells.

Overhead cameras could see every commode on the block. It was humiliating to know someone might be watching every time I took a shit and wiped my ass.

On our pod, we showered eight at a time in a common stall. The guards hurried us through in two minutes or less. I tried not to think about what would happen if an inmate saw me in the shower and liked what he saw. Since it was impossible to know what was going through the minds of sex-deprived inmates, I tried to hide myself as best as I could. I avoided looking at anyone, not even a glance, and I was careful not to accidentally touch anybody or let anybody touch me. Stories circulated of how jail turns straight guys into homos, and I didn't want anybody on the down low thinking I was pretty. When you're young and "white and tight," you're careful. When you're in the shower, you don't drop the soap.

Razors were kept locked at the guard station and were signed out and checked in after each shave. For security reasons, all the blades were accounted for. I was allowed to keep my toothbrush in the cell, along with writing paper and other limited incidentals I purchased at the commissary. The fortunate inmates opened a commissary account. Most purchased crackers, letter envelopes, cigarettes, and candy. Lucky for me, I got arrested on the way to Pittsburgh to buy drugs. This allowed me to fund my commissary account with the $400 I was planning to spend for a brick of heroin.

I did my laundry once a week. That doesn't mean I went to a washing machine in the jail and washed my dirty clothes. It means I put my allotted three pairs of underwear and socks in a mesh bag with my tag on it and tossed it in the bin as it rolled by the cell each Tuesday afternoon. The bags were returned any day between Wednesday and Friday. I couldn't stand wearing dirty underwear, and so half the time I would "free ball" it until the clean underwear came back. Most weeks Jordan slept through laundry pickup.

Inmates were allowed to make collect telephone calls from the jail during specified hours. All calls were monitored by a guard wearing a headset, standing behind. There weren't enough guards or phones for each prisoner, so the more savvy inmates, or the stronger ones, were first in line. A skinny guy like me had no chance to use a phone, and I never did. Incoming calls were restricted to family emergencies or legal matters. Getting summoned off the block to the telephones never happened to me and rarely happened to any of the others. The corrections officers were too busy with necessary tasks to take the time to escort an inmate for a phone call.

Almost immediately, depression set in. I wondered if I

could survive in this indoor wasteland. No plants. No fresh air. No sunshine. Outside light searched for a way into the prison and found its way through slender three-inch wide smoky glass panels. By looking at the glass from inside, I could tell if it was daylight or dark, that's all. I never knew if it was hot outside, or raining, or snowing. Constant temperatures and fluorescent lights insured that inside conditions were always the same. I longed for fresh air, the warmth of the sun, a cool breeze, and all that the outside world offered. I missed watching girls walk through the mall dressed in hot clothes. And when they passed, how they would look over their shoulder to see if I saw what they wanted me to see.

We were permitted to roam around the activity hall during rec time. The room was equipped with five stationary card tables, some checker boards, and a television. Occasionally, a card game would break out. Among prisoners, the favorite was a four-handed game called spades. At home, I watched my dad and uncles play bridge with my grandma so I knew how to play cards even though I couldn't play bridge. Spades was much simpler, and in two weeks time I became a spades shark.

The television was mounted overhead where it could be viewed from three corners of the room. A remote control device lay on a table, but everyone knew not to change channels. The Big Dog took care of that. We watched what the Big Dog wanted to watch. We let the Big Dog eat.

I tried to be careful not do anything that would make enemies. Making friends was impossible. There was no trust in the prison setting. It was every man for himself. Although we all shared space and time and routine, we never developed a spirit of camaraderie like serving in the Army or on a sports team. What little bonding that took place in jail happened along racial lines and was not forged out of common sweat and brotherhood. Blacks quickly bonded with other blacks, and whites with whites. I don't mean to suggest there were racial problems in jail. I just couldn't figure out why persons of the same race chose to hang with each other over persons of a different race, especially where the chosen friend was an asshole–and there was no shortage of assholes in jail, black or white.

After six or seven days, the harsh effects of withdrawal wore off, and my head cleared enough for me to write a letter to my dad. My spelling was poor, and I wrote run-on sentences with no paragraphing. I am one of those who could talk better than he could write. Who would have thought if I had made more of an effort to learn language skills in school my time in jail would be better? Now, when I needed to write, I struggled.

Dad wrote several letters to me during those two months in prison. His message was consistent. Dad told me that I was a special person in God's eyes, and that God had a plan for me, but that only I could discover what that plan was. I liked hearing that I was special and that God was interested in my life, even though I wasn't sure if I believed in God. Being told you are special makes you feel good. It would make anyone feel good.

I was a piece of shit. Everyone needs to be loved, I

suppose, but why would anybody love me. I had done absolutely nothing in my life to deserve love. Does love have to be earned–or, is it an entitlement of personhood?

I grew up with my family telling my brother Ben and me that we were special because we were adopted. I never really accepted this theory lock, stock, and barrel the way Ben did. To me, there was nothing special about being given up at birth. Part of me still believes that if my birth mother really wanted me, she would have kept me. As it stands, I would like to know more about the circumstances of her decision to give me away, but at the same time, I don't care to make any inquiries.

When we were little, my brother Ben and I loved to hear the story of our adoptions. Our little faces brightened when we learned about how it all happened. About how in mid-May, 1981, when I was four months old, Catholic Social Services Agency completed their search for suitable parents and placed me. About how I was brought home with straps holding my legs in an outward position because I had dislocated a hip at birth. About how Dad and Mom boarded a jet airplane one week later and picked up Ben at the Los Angeles Airport terminal when he was just two days old. About how they had to run, carrying tiny Ben from one concourse to another in order to catch their return flight, which allowed them only a two-hour turnaround time. About how, at first, they thought Ben was a Mexican because he came from California and had a red face and greasy black hair. About how Ben wouldn't sleep and kept Mom and Dad awake with his piercing "wah-wah" cry.

We both enjoyed hearing about all of the friends and relatives who came to see us when we first arrived home. You can imagine the fuss around our house! More than 300 people stopped to see us, most bringing gifts. Friends and relatives drove around the block until a parking space opened up in our driveway, then they pulled in. When I was little, hearing that story made me feel good. It still makes me feel good. That story would make anyone feel good. I don't care who you are.

One thing I wasn't feeling good about was being in jail. I don't imagine my family felt good about it either. Thankfully, they were spared the sight of seeing me lying on my cot covered with vomit.

Many experts in penology believe that the most punishing aspect of incarceration is the loss of dignity. This would be true only if the convict were truly innocent of the crime for which he was sentenced. For those of us who were rightfully in jail, our dignity was surrendered the moment the crime was committed.

My theory about the punitive aspect of jail differs from that of the so-called experts who most likely never spent a single night behind bars. I believe jail punishes a person because it deprives him of the ability to allocate time. The freedom to decide what to do and when to do it is never appreciated until it is taken away. Sometimes in life time is of the essence. In jail, it never is, but at the same time, it always is. When you are behind bars, others tell you what to do. Others decide when you will do it. This is punishment. That is how it is in jail.

With time on my hands, I did some thinking. I hated myself and decided to reform my life forever as soon as I got out of prison. Drugs would not deprive me of a good family life. I would not risk jail again just to get high, and I vowed to never again allow drugs to enslave me. I was determined to live as God's child and discover the special plan He had for me.

Even though my resolve to change my life was firm, at some level deep in my being I sensed a weakness, as if the conscious part of me were being overtaken by a sinister subconscious force. Already the darker side of my brain started to stir. The sound of distant drums began beating that irrepressible cadence which tempted me to pick up – again. Things were happening over which I had no control.

CHAPTER TWO
Dancing with Death

It was the last Friday of February 2003. A cold winter day on the outside, but not cold, not winter on the inside. The guard approached me as I sat with my plastic lunch tray finishing a dry hamburger. "Grab your stuff, Weaver. You're getting out of here." The look on the corrections officer's face told me this was no prank; he was serious. I was being discharged from prison, but I didn't understand why I was being let out so soon. Court papers had me scheduled to go before the judge for sentencing on April 11th. Why, I wondered, would they release me before then.

For a second, I thought my dad was behind this, but I dismissed that thought. I had disappointed him too many times, and after getting caught with dope again, I was sure he had given up on me. Dad wouldn't even post my bond. My early release probably was the result of some obscure law or a procedural quirk that worked to my benefit. The legal system was confusing to me, and the more I thought about it, the more confused I became. One thing was clear to me, my early release had nothing to do with my being special. To the Warden, I was just another swinging dick taking up space in his overcrowded jail.

No matter the reasons for my leaving, I was ready, and I never wanted to return. We walked to my cell, and I collected my stack of letters, toothbrush, and the Michael Crichton book I was reading, "The Lost World," and stuffed these items into a plastic bag the corrections officer had just given me. Thankfully, Jordan was still at lunch when I left. In two months' time we hardly spoke to each other, and I had no interest in saying goodbye to that loser. What I wanted to do was stuff Jordan's shaved head down that steel commode he sat on so much of the time.

The guard took me to out-processing where I changed into the street clothes I was wearing when Officer Schellhammer arrested me. As I pulled on the oversized sweatshirt, I noticed it fit better. So did the baggy pants. Two months of working out in my room and eating a high carbohydrate diet at regular times added 40 pounds of rock hard muscle to my frame.

Exercising was a good way to pass the time and build self-esteem. There were no weight training facilities in the prison. So I improvised by putting books in my pillow case for weights and did arm curls. For shoulders, I did pushups until I could perform 100 repetitions. To build the upper part of my chest, I elevated my feet on the cot and did decline pushups. My body looked better than it ever looked, and I couldn't wait to do a little showing off for the girls. Another thing, I was no longer afraid of Jordan. Which I didn't want to be.

After I changed into civies, the officer placed four or five separate papers before me for my signature. He explained they were releases–from what I didn't know. The only release I was concerned about was the one that would let me pass through the sliding door to the outside world. The officer pressed his finger on each paper showing me where to sign. I signed them all without reading a single word.

I was escorted up the steps and dropped in the holding cell where I sat on the same hardwood bench as when I entered two months earlier. Compared to the Adam Weaver who shuffled into the jail on Christmas Eve, the man who was about to stride out was a changed person. Most noticeable were the physical changes. I was bigger, stronger, healthier.

Changes took place on the inside as well. My outlook was brighter, if for no other reason than when I looked in a mirror, I did not see a hang-dog, slump-shouldered recluse. The mirror reflected back a person with potential. With time for self-examination, I promised myself I would not backslide into the world of needles and syringes, where every waking moment is spent wondering when I would score my next buy, how I would get money, which friend would go to jail next, which friend would die. Drugs were a part of my past, not my future. Which was how it should be.

Nervously, I waited on the bench. Still, nobody offered an explanation of why I was getting out of jail early. Asking the CO's would be pointless. Their job was to out-process the con from "G-37," not offer severance counseling. Let well enough alone, I figured.

I started thinking about where I would go when I hit the street and how I would get there. Most likely, Dad would have already sold my Ford Explorer. Why should he keep up insurance payments when I couldn't drive the vehicle anyway? Besides, the Explorer was titled in his name. He bought it for me so I would have transportation to work, but in the past three years, I couldn't hold any job for more than a couple of months.

Once released, I didn't know where I could find money to buy food, or where I'd sleep, or get warm clothes. How would I get a job? Without wheels, I had no way to get to work. I needed Tegretol to control my seizures and I had no money to buy those expensive pills. All these thoughts were piling up on me. A non-withdrawal headache set in. I decided not to over worry and just deal with each issue as it popped up, one at a time. On the one hand, I was ready to leave, but on the other hand I wasn't. While I was behind bars, I didn't need to concern myself with how I was going to get life's necessities. The County handled those problems. On the outside, the problems were mine.

At last, I heard the electronic clicks that triggered the door mechanism. It slid open. Through the doorway I could see my dad standing on the other side. "Let's go home, Adam." was all he said. My father had come for me. Dad had not given up on me after all! In my heart, I believed that he would take care of me and try to help me. I was getting another chance to live at home with Dad and Ben where I would have a warm and safe place to sleep. As we walked to the car, Dad put his arm around my shoulder as if to say, "Son, let's try again."

All my life, I have been hiding. I never let myself express emotions like love, or hope, or fear. Sometimes I could laugh and smile, but mostly I remained emotionally aloof. For that matter, my stoicism carried over to the suppression of physical feelings as well. My movements lacked animation even under circumstances which called for some excitement. In times of pain, I hid behind a shield of toughness.

I remember breaking my arm while playing roller hockey as an 11-year-old. Before setting the bone, Dr. Trevor Yardley numbed the area with lidocaine by sticking a long needle into the bone right where it had broken. It hurt a lot, but the only pains I showed were a few flinches, which I couldn't hold back.

Three years ago when Pap died, I attended the funeral events because it was expected of me, not because I wanted to be there. My cousins came from out of town, but I stayed away as much as I could so I wouldn't need to interact with any of them or explain my sorry life to them. Listening to Kevin brag that he was second in his class studying electrical engineering only served to remind me of my own underachievements, and I didn't give a shit whether Elaine had one master's degree in chemistry or ten of them. Feelings of shame were slowly, subtly, and surely grinding down what little self-esteem I had left.

Not once during the entire funeral observance did I approach my dad or any of my uncles and offer my support. Not once did I join my family for meals or prayer. Always I remained on the fringe of the circle, afraid to join hands with the rest.

No one could have asked for a better grandma or pap than I got, but when Grandma needed me, I disappeared. I suppressed the impulses to run to Grandma and comfort her and tell her how grateful I was for all the good things Pap had done for me in his life. All my happy memories of Pap should have been shared with Grandma; memories of him delivering scrap wood in his old pickup truck so I could build my back yard cabin; memories of Pap cursing when he locked the keys in his car; memories of Pap dressed in a black tuxedo greeting guests at his 60th wedding anniversary party. We should have reminisced about Pap giving me a ride home from hockey practice or guitar lessons when Dad couldn't. I should have told Grandma how much I loved Pap.

Drugging numbed the emotional part of me. I thought of myself only as a physical person, without realizing all of us, including me, are partly spiritual and partly physical. In fact, after spending a two-month dope-free stint in jail, I began to see persons more as spiritual creatures than physical ones. Two months in a striped suit taught me that the differences among persons lie not in their height, weight, age, or sex, but rather in the things you can't touch or weigh or measure.

While I recognized the need to be more open with myself and with others, something cautioned me not to get close or involved with any of the inmates. In jail, I was forced to shower with strangers, eat with strangers, even use the bathroom in the presence of strangers. I was in the company of hundreds of people all the time, but I never felt more alone. The loneliness of prison in the constant presence of strangers is not as bad as the loneliness of addiction in the presence of loved ones.

On the drive home we stopped at an Eat-N-Park restaurant where I ordered a Mountain Man platter. Between bites, Dad and I discussed living arrangements. It was understood and agreed that I could move back home and that I would begin the process of choosing a vocation. Dad was trying to guide me toward a higher education, either college or a trade school. He explained that an education was not only a way to earn a better living but would also enhance the quality of my life through knowledge and understanding. Once obtained, no one could take my education away from me. The choice was mine. Whatever road I took, he would help me reach the destination. Now that I was thinking with a clear head, I pleaded for a bit of time to sort through the options. Which was fine with Dad.

While I was in jail, Dad had begun a total basement remodeling project. Everything was gutted down to the block walls and floor joists. What a mess! Weeks of plumbing, wiring, framing, and finish work lay ahead. No need waiting for Dad to tell me what to do. I could see what had to be done. Besides, working up a sweat would provide a constructive outlet for my new-found energies and buy time to contemplate my future. For the first time in a long while, the situation at home between Dad and me was win-win.

It had been two months since I slept in a real bed, my own bed. The sleep was sound and deep. There were no clanging doors, no range lights, and no sights or sounds or smells from Jordan.

Sleeping past my intentions, I got out of bed late Saturday morning. The coffee should have been brewed and the newspaper on the table when Dad got awake, but it didn't happen that way. Instead, when I walked down the stairs from my bedroom, I heard power tools humming in the basement and smelled the coffee Dad had already brewed. Two slices of toast spread with Smuckers all natural peanut butter was enough breakfast for me. I hurried to the basement, tied on a tool belt, and helped Dad nail tongue-and-grooved knotty pine paneling boards for approximately 40 minutes.

My chance came when we ran out of boards and Dad sent me to Lowe's to buy more. He handed me his wallet so I would have money to pay. Immediately upon backing Dad's car out of the driveway, I was no longer in control of my choices. Something more powerful than free will had its hands on the steering wheel. I took what Dad would call a "frolic and detour," and drove to a friend's house to pick up four packets of heroin for $25 each. Probably I could have talked my friend down to $20 a bag, but my friend hooked me up with a rig for the same money. And I knew Dad wouldn't miss an even $100 from his wallet.

It was so easy to steal from my father. Dad never knew how much money he had in his wallet at any given time and often left it lying on top of the microwave or on the dresser in his room, which was right around the corner from mine. I disciplined myself and was careful not to oversteal. Taking smaller amounts at frequent intervals proved to be the safest way to insure the money wasn't missed. Moreover, Dad was the consummate trusting soul. If I heard him say it once, I heard him say a thousand times that he would not be a prisoner in his own castle, nor would he live under conditions where he kept his property under lock and key. Dad's principles served him well. They served me even better.

On Monday, I drove Dad to his law office since I needed the car to get more building materials for the basement project. As I dropped him off, I asked for a few bucks for smokes and incidentals. I got a $20 bill to go along with the credit card Dad gave me to use at Lowe's. By now, the distant drums were sounding nearer. After dropping Dad off, I went on another "frolic and detour." At my friend's house, we dumped the white powder onto a spoon, and we mixed it with water and drew it into the syringe. An old brown belt was tightened around our upper arms until our veins popped out. A few minutes later, we got well. It was that easy.

When Dad was at the office, I did just enough work in the basement to make him think I was pitching in as best as I could. I shot just enough heroin to take me down without causing me to be so dazed that Dad might notice when he got home. One of the things Dad checked to determine if I was using was the size of my pupils. When I was "on," my pupils were no bigger than a pin head and wouldn't dilate. He had an uncanny ability for detecting when I was high on dope. Therefore, I tried to stay away from Dad when I used, which was every day.

On Wednesday, Dad and I planned to meet at his office at 5 p.m. We intended to go out for dinner followed by a Chiefs hockey game. When I failed to show up with the car at five, Dad called his cell phone, which he was letting me use so he could track me down. After several unanswered calls, Dad walked to the By George Inn to bum a ride home from one of the patrons. His young associate attorney, David Raho, happened to be there.

Raho's Honda pulled into our driveway at 5:47 p.m. The garage door was open. Dad's green Beamer sat inside. Oddly, my second floor bedroom light was lit.

I never heard them enter the home. Dad and Dave thought I must have lost track of time while working on the remodeling project. They went directly to the basement searching for me. When they couldn't find me, Dad began calling out, "Adam!" Finally, they walked up to my bedroom. They found me on the bed, lying on my back, left arm stretched out. Small amounts of blood had dried on the inside of my left elbow, right where I stuck the needles.

Decomposition started almost immediately after my heart and lungs stopped. My body turned cold to the touch. Skin faded to an ashen color and began to blacken around the lips and around the eye sockets. Limbs stiffened in early stage rigor mortis. By all appearances, I was dead!

While I was in prison, my body lost its tolerance to drugs. Now I wasn't able to take a hit like when I was using regularly. For me, ten or more bags of heroin a day was normal. There was a span of several months where I topped out with as many as 30 bags of heroin each day. Against that background of heavy use, I thought I could take two bumps, no problem. The little packets I tore open had all the usual street stamps, and I had every reason to suspect the stuff I was soon going to shoot had already been "cut." Had I known it was nearly laboratory pure, I would have cut it myself with ordinary flour or baby powder.

The first shot made me feel better. The second got me in trouble. Silently, the dope coursed its way through my blood stream and into my central nervous system. My heartbeat relaxed and my breathing quieted until it was slow; then slower still; then nothing. I passed through the comatose stage restfully and calmed, fading inexorably toward a peaceful death.

Dad checked for a pulse at my neck, then my wrist, and finally my feet. There was none. He lifted my eyelids and saw nothing but whites. I guess your eyes roll back into your head when you die. Dave Raho had the presence of mind to run downstairs and grab the telephone to dial 911. By the time he got back upstairs to my bedroom, Dad was feverishly working on me.

"Wake up, Adam!" he boomed. "Come on Adam. Stay awake!" Without wasting another breath, Dad blew my air passages clear. A thick whitish substance was expelled from my nostrils and flew onto the bed sheets. For the first time in a long while, my chest heaved with air. Leaning over the bed for leverage, Dad thumped my chest with the back of his fist directly on the sternum. Then he brought all his weight to bear on my breast bone, rhythmically pressing, one hand on top of the other, trying against all odds to squeeze life into my body. By rights my chest plate should have snapped under the force of such heavy compressions, but for some reason the bones held. Getting my heart pumping far outweighed the risk of breaking bones.

In desperation, Dad performed a maneuver not written in medical books or taught in CPR classes. He grabbed me under the arms and lifted me to my feet, dancing me like a rag doll across the room, then twirling me back to my bed. Dad hoped this tango would get the blood circulating throughout my body by moving it mechanically through the one-way valves in my legs. With an open hand Dad slapped all over my chest and face, figuring these sharp stings might stimulate a brain response. They didn't. My body lay limp, but there was no quit in my father. The CPR efforts continued without let up, blow by blow, pump by pump. I had finally found peace in my tormented life, and now, if only Dad would let me alone, I could enjoy the death that was waiting for me.

Six or seven minutes later, my right eyelid opened for just an instant. My pupil rolled down into proper alignment, then as quickly as it had dropped, it returned back into the top of my head. Dad took his thumb and lifted my eyelid, but it still showed a white out. This caused him to reason that my earlier wink was merely a reflex and not a true sign of life.

At this point, Dad's thoughts were to open my chest with a pair of scissors he kept in the bathroom and massage my heart manually, but this drastic measure would be deferred until he checked one final time for an outward sign of life. He placed his right hand around my neck as if to choke me and then gently tightened his grip. There was a faint pulse!

Dad shouted, "Wake up, Adam! Wake up! You can come back, Adam! Come on back, Adam!"

There must have been an Invisible Hand showing Dad exactly what to do. No one should have been able to survive when they were as far gone as I was. I don't care who you are.

East Mountain Ambulance was en route to the station house with a full crew of trained EMT's when orders came over the radio at 6:27 p.m. to respond to a residence for a "drug overdose with possible death." Raho's call had gotten through. At 6:34 p.m., four blue-suited paramedics clogged upstairs with their boots and portable life saving machines to take over the resuscitation work. I was intubated, placed on a stretcher, and taken to Central Hospital, unconscious but breathing. Which was more than anyone could have hoped.

Only Mortals Can Be Heroes

CHAPTER   THREE

Beginnings

The telephone rang at Uncle Dan's house.   "Hello." answered Dad's twin brother.

"Daniel, is there any chance of you meeting me at Central Hospital? Adam overdosed again."

"Oh, no! Oh, no!"

"He wasn't breathing when I found him. Don't know how long he was lying on his bed before I got to him. Anyway, I'd like to talk to you, if you can possibly get away." Sounding deadpan was Dad's understated way of expressing the gravity of my condition.

"Are you in the hospital now?" asked Uncle Dan.

"I'm in the Emergency Room. They've got Adam hooked up to all sorts of machines. There is an overhead monitor with an oscillating white line across, but I don't know what that measures. He has a blood pressure cuff, a clip on his index finger, oxygen tubes in his nose, a catheter, an IV line stuck on the back side of his wrist, and a big tube down his throat." Dad was trying to be factual, but even he could not hide the anxiety in his voice. "Daniel, this one might be touch and go. Adam did not look too good when he was loaded into the ambulance. You'll find us." said my father as he pressed the red button to disconnect the cell phone, and waited for his twin brother to meet him downtown.

Within 15 minutes Uncle Dan arrived. He came right to the point. "What do you mean? 'Adam overdosed again.' Did he overdose before?" he queried.

Dad explained that five years earlier, I had indeed been taken to the hospital for a drug overdose, but that one was from cocaine, not heroin. The year was 1998. It was the summer between my junior and senior years in high school. I was hanging around with teenaged neighborhood kids, most of whom I knew all my life. We met playing pee wee hockey, at the playground, or riding dirt bikes. Over the years I made a lot of friends, and all came from upper-middle class families.

We were 16 or 17 years old then, and our activities had changed. A select group of four or five of my buddies would often get together to snort coke. We became brazen and snorted in the presence of nonusers. Those who wouldn't do a line had become so accustomed to watching us who did, that seeing friends get high was no big deal. There was no need to hide our drug activities. Snorting coke became a social event, even though I preferred to do coke by myself. If girls were involved, we usually smoked a little pot first. This loosened their inhibitions, making them willing partakers of almost any follow up drug activity.

Sometimes we smoked crack. Crack is a processed form of cocaine. It is produced by cooking powder cocaine in secret labs or at home until it solidifies, like when Grandma cooks candy to the hardball stage. After hardening, the substance is broken into little pieces called rocks, which are dropped into a pipe bowl and lit. Generally you could only get one hit out of a small piece of crack, but that was enough for a good rush.

Any high school student could buy crack in the school bathrooms from other students for as little as $10 a rock. But, since in-school buys were risky, most crack deals were transacted off school property. Older students who could drive automobiles hooked up by driving to any of the public housing sections of town and waiting in their cars to be hit on by one of the ever-present crack dealers, usually a black dude.

My romance with drugs began during the summer between seventh and eight grades under circumstances nobody would have suspected. One of my favorite outlets was working with hand tools. These tools were put to good use when I decided to build a cabin in the woods behind my house. My brother, Ben, helped some, but he was more interested in playing golf. Neighborhood kids showed up to help, especially as the shanty took shape. Soon I had an impressive undertaking on my hands, with plenty of volunteer labor.

A large beech tree had fallen across Sam's Run, which meanders along the back of our property. That fallen tree served as the skeleton for a ramshackle structure that eventually became a two-story hangout. It was neat. When the beech tree fell to the ground, it did not completely flatten. Some of the higher branches arched across the brook, forming an irregular scaffold upon which we framed our tree house.

Our gang of adolescents scrounged around the neighborhood and brought back boards of all sizes that we nailed across the crescent shaped higher branches of the downed tree. This resulted in a shed type roof which we covered with rolled roofing paper that Pap supplied from leftovers garnered during his years as a contractor. For walls, we busted the pallets Pap delivered and nailed the boards everywhere and anywhere they fit, in a helter-skelter pattern. Then we tarpapered the outside walls for weatherproofing.

For light and air, we cut out two windows and left an entrance on the upstream side. A chicken ladder connected ground level to the second floor. The upper deck was constructed with larger boards we nailed directly to the stronger tree limbs in a hit-and-miss arrangement. Dad had just installed indoor/outdoor carpeting on the back porch of our house. We dragged the old green carpet away from the garbage pickup pile and used it to cover the ground floor in our hut. After weeks of hard work, we assumed occupancy.

In no time our little bungalow in the woods became an attraction for older boys. Someone came up with the appealing notion to leave a small opening from the second floor directly over the creek. That way it would be easy to retrieve a six pack of beer, which was kept chilled in the cool stream below. Tying beer to the end of a rope and dipping the beer into the cool stream wasn't my idea. My friend, Matt's older brother, Jerry, deserves credit for that brainstorm. It was also Jerry who gave us weed for the first time, which we smoked in the hideout. From the time Jerry first introduced me to dope and suds, I was smoking weed and drinking beer every day. At 12 years of age, I took to marijuana and beer like the crawfish took to Sam's Run.

It is ironic that the first time I smoked pot and drank beer was in a shack I built as a form of therapy to counteract depression. Little did I know, and never could have I anticipated, that working on a cabin during my summer of innocence would lead to the corruption of my young life.

There were, however, plenty of pleasant firsts in my life. And I remember them well. For instance, I remember the first time Dad took me and Ben to Hidden Valley Ski Resort. I was terrified and thrilled at the same time.

I remember my excitement when Mom and Dad took us to City Cycle to pick out our first two-wheelers. I chose a blue bike, and Ben decided on a red one.

How could I ever forget my first little league home run! It was an inside-the-parker. I ran as fast as my little legs could churn around second base, but stopped at third. Coach yelled, "Run, Adam, run! Keep going, Adam!" I bolted the final 60 feet and slid into home, not knowing that poor Aaron Pejak had muffed the ball in short right field and didn't even try to peg me out at the plate. After the game, Coach presented me with the baseball I smashed for the home run. What wonderful memories I have of the privileged childhood I enjoyed!

In contrast, I have a few memories of my childhood which I wish I could block out, like the first time I pulled on a joint in the cabin, and the first time I snapped an aluminum top on a can of Coors Light. Regrettably, my mind contains these memories no matter how hard I try to pour them out.

By the time I was 11 years old, Ben and I got $15 weekly allowances. This must have been the going rate in suburbia at the time, because nearly all of our friends received the same stipend. Fifteen bucks allowed me to purchase marijuana. For extra money, I began to steal cigarettes from a local convenience store and sell them at school. With no cost of acquisition, all the money I got from the sale of these stolen smokes was profit.

Meanwhile, Matt and I joined a group of punks and vandals who called themselves, "The Green Knights." As our need for money increased, we gang members became more creative with our chicanery. One caper was quite clever. We dressed up my friend, T.J., like a Boy Scout and dispatched him door to door to sell pies. T.J. took orders for pies which were to be delivered at a later date. We stung approximately 60 unsuspecting donors for more than $400 on that one day with the pic gig. Another time we bought candy bars from the Ideal grocery store at three for $1.00 and sold them at $1.00 a piece telling folks that we were raising money for Boy Scout summer camp.

There was a certain rebelliousness inside me that had to come out. I got a thrill out of breaking the law. Since I never fit in with the hip crowd, disobeying the law was one way I could demonstrate superiority over those too chicken to risk getting caught doing something illegal. We Green Knights repeatedly broke the law. Being a gang member provided the perfect opportunity to vent my rebellious nature.

Other misfits a few years older than me were doing even

harder drugs. These guys led me through a natural progression from marijuana to other types of illegal substances, including cocaine and heroin. Booze and pot served as warm-ups paving the way for other drugs. By 14 years of age, I was ready to move on to stronger stuff.

It was during my freshman year in high school that I began experimenting with hard drugs. A fellow Knight, Brian, told me he had hits of LSD in his book bag. That day was a short Friday, when school let out at noon. We met in the school restroom, and each of us licked a hit from the blotter paper during class change at 9:52. By the time school was dismissed, I was tripping my balls off.

As I floated down the hall, the walls closed in on me. Everyone's voice echoed in my head and reverberated as if the hallways had transformed into a concert hall. A kaleidoscope of nonexistent objects appeared across my brain. These bizarre hallucinations were not enough to satisfy my insatiable thirst for a greater thrill. So when I got home from school, I smoked a joint on top of the acid. Euphoria rushed at me from all angles.

All through high school, I hit the blotter paper on a regular basis and never took a bad trip. Acid became my high school sweetheart. Oh, how we could dance!

Another of my favorite drugs was Ritalin, a medicine prescribed to calm persons who are hyperactive. My friend, Conner, was taking Ritalin ever since he started elementary school. By the time Conner and I were in the tenth grade, he was selling his Ritalin to me.

According to the label on the medicine bottle, Ritalin was to be administered in tablet form once in the morning and once in the afternoon. Following these directions would have resulted in hardly any desirable effect, because the release action would have been too slow. Therefore, I wrapped a dollar bill around the tablets and pulverized them into powder with a cigarette lighter, one tablet at a time. A couple of quick snorts later, and it was off to the wild blue yonder for the better part of an hour. The view from above was more pleasing to me than sitting in a classroom trying to learn algebra.

Much of the summer of my tenth grade, I spent at my friend, Burt's, house. Almost every day a group of us Knights would smoke dope and drink beer. I tried "schrooms" which made me feel crazy or goofy for long periods of time. I even did "Dust Off," an aerosol computer cleaner we bought at Staples. My friends and I would discharge the chemical into a plastic bag and breathe it, holding our breath for maximum uptake. This made me feel as though I was going to pass out. Once I moved beyond the unpleasant smell, I was rewarded with a feeling of being in an altered state. We all did a lot of "huffing" that summer at Burt's.

With friends around for support, I would do whatever drug was put in front of me. Nothing frightened me. When it came to drugs, I could match any friend: snort for snort, puff for puff, huff for huff. It didn't matter whether we did alcohol, Ecstasy, marijuana, cocaine, heroin, Ritalin, crystal meth, speed balls, LSD, pain pills, downers, uppers, and everything in-between. When you're trying to fit in with your friends, you do whatever they do. Nobody wants to be called a pussy.

I don't care who you are.

Throughout my high school years, my drug of choice was cocaine. Whether I smoked crack or snorted cocaine powder, the effect on me was the same. The rush hit quickly and took me way up. Every sensory organ in my body functioned at supernormal capacity. My eyesight was so sharp I thought at times I could see right through objects and beyond them. Ordinary conversation produced powerful resonant sounds, as if the vibes were coming out of the boom box Ben and I hooked up in the back of our first car, a '92 Pontiac Grand Am. The surface of my skin became so tactile that I believed I could actually reach out and touch another person's breath. For a few minutes when I was high, I could escape from the dungeon in which I dwelled and allow the chemical reactions going on in my brain to work their magic. When I was wired, I felt like a new man. Things were wonderful!

Cocaine is a powerful central nervous system stimulant. Most addicts describe the cocaine high as an incredibly intense total body orgasm. Which it is. The problems begin when you start to come down. This occurs 20 or 30 minutes into the experience. You remember the high you just had, so you chase it with more drugs, and still more. Each succeeding hit produces an incrementally smaller rush. After so much pounding and abuse, your brain receptors throw up their hands and say, "We give up. We're overloaded." Then you convulse. That's what happened to me when I overdosed in the summer of 1998. I was just 17.

To this day, I'm not certain whether cocaine was the sole cause of that overdose. I had been snorting cocaine for more than two years and never had a problem. Make no mistake about it, even though I was young, I was a seasoned veteran. However, cocaine is unpredictable. You can be cruising real high, line after line; then–boom! Down you go.

Most likely I spazzed out from a seizure disorder I have had since I was six or seven years old. These days people seem to be afraid to call my condition epilepsy, but that's what I think I have. Doctors prescribed Tegretol, to prevent seizures, but sometimes I would miss a dose or two. When I felt depressed, I didn't care what happened to me, and I just skipped my pills for the day. I don't remember whether I took my Tegretol on the day I overdosed or not, probably not. In my mind, more than likely it was the dangerous combination of using a lot of cocaine and skipping my Tegretol that took me down.

Dr. Fred Munzer was on duty at the hospital the night I arrived by ambulance. Dr. Fred is our next door neighbor and has been my doctor all my life. He knows my body like his own son's. Since he knew about my epilepsy, the first thing he did was run a blood check to determine Tegretol levels. They were low. When the Emergency Room nurse informed Dr. Fred that the drug screen also showed positive for cocaine, he knew exactly how to treat me. I'm not saying I would have died if Dr. Fred had not been on call that evening. I'm just saying I could not have hand-picked any doctor who knew my condition as intimately as Dr. Fred. Indeed, I lived a charmed life.

I was in and out of consciousness while the nurses got their lines in me. Sometimes I felt the sticks, sometimes I didn't. I'll never forget the nurses trying to collect the urine specimen so they could run a drug screen to find out what substances were in my system. Ordinarily, getting a specimen presents no problem. However, one of the side effects of cocaine is the inability to urinate. Another is dryness. Dry skin, dry mouth. Cocaine also acts as a constrictor, tightening the body's vessels. That was exactly my condition, tight and dry. Never was there a candidate less suited for catheterizing. If you want to know all there is to know about pain, I invite you to get catheterized right after a cocaine bender. I can tough anything out, but when the nurses started working me over, I lost it. The pain was like an orgasm in reverse, except worse.

My situation got more complicated when an MRI of my head revealed I was walking around with a brain tumor the size of a ping pong ball, situated in the left temporal region. The report called it a glioma. To make matters worse, the hospital wouldn't discharge me until they did additional testing to learn more about this glioma.

Dr. Musef, the hospital neurologist, was called upon to examine me. He was 6' 3" and weighed at least 250 pounds, having hands the size of dinner plates. Quite obviously, Dr. Musef deserved his nickname, "Moose." With hands as big as his, it would not surprise me if he could change a tire on his automobile without a lug wrench. What I wondered was whether Dr. Musef had sufficient dexterity to skillfully maneuver a tiny medical instrument during a delicate brain procedure.

Dr. Musef began the examination by looking into my eyes

and shining that thin light beam that ought to make you squint but doesn't. Then he took a small rubber mallet and tapped my knees making my legs jump. He jabbed me with pins at sensitive parts of my body, and I felt every one of the pin points. Dr. Musef extended two of his sausage-sized fingers for me to squeeze with both hands, which I did, proving my strength was good bilaterally. Then he watched me touch the tip of my nose with both of my index fingers and walk heel to toe like a drunk driver taking a field sobriety test. I passed the neurological exam and figured that was the end of my glioma worries, but it wasn't.

A day later I got word that "Moose" was planning to drill my head to biopsy the tumor so he could find out if it was cancerous. My dad put a stop to those plans, real quick. I was glad he did. We both figured since I had no symptoms, let it alone. To this day, I don't know whether my tumor is going to act up or not. So far, so good.

Now, nearly five years later, here I was again in an emergency room because of a drug overdose. Two and a half hours ticked off the clock while Uncle Dan and my dad sat anxiously waiting for me to respond. They cornered the charge nurse, seeking reassurances from her that I would soon break out of my coma. All she would tell them was, "Sometimes they come out of these things just fine, sometimes there are complications."

To Dad and Uncle Dan, the word "complications" meant brain damage. What else could it mean? From all he could observe, Dad already concluded that my chance of ever living a normal life was slim.

"You just told me what happened the time Adam overdosed on cocaine, but tonight didn't he get too much heroin?" questioned Uncle Dan, struggling to clear his confusion concerning which drugs I used and when. My dad reiterated that, yes, the present overdose was from heroin, but the previous OD was from cocaine. At this point, it was Uncle Dan's brain receptors that were on the verge of overloading. As smart as he was, Uncle Dan could only assimilate so much in a limited period of time. He had just completed a crash course on street drugs while sitting in a hospital waiting room. It was time to stop the information bombardment.

Uncle Dan and my dad grew up at a time when the worst thing that could have happened to a guy was getting some girl knocked up. The big question of their day was, "Did you use a rubber?" Back in the 50's and 60's, children weren't fat, neighbors knew each other, video games were nonexistent, and sensitivity training consisted of a kick in the ass from your dad. Uncle Dan was a social dinosaur, but I loved him. He had no idea that several of my friends had already been sentenced to jail terms for drug-related crimes, or that five had died from dope; four boys and one girl. In the good old days, drug-related deaths were rare. Today they are commonplace.

My dad continued the conversation, "Daniel, as best I could determine, Adam got into heroin in his senior year in high school or shortly after that. One night I received a telephone call out of the blue from a girl who told me that Adam had begun injecting heroin. You can imagine how that made me feel."

"Did the girl give her name?"

"Yes, she did, but only after I promised not to disclose her identity. The girl said she was a heroin user and had gone away for treatment, but she was still scared to death. She said after she got hooked on heroin, she couldn't stand the thought of living without it, and she couldn't stand the thought of living with it."

"Must be bad stuff. Did she ever call again?" asked Uncle Dan.

"No, but I remember she was a real nice girl who was still struggling. I thanked her for calling. The girl said she would pray for Adam."

Dad's timetable was correct. My love-hate relationship with heroin began late in my senior year. Actually, it was very near the time of graduation. Before then, I had snorted heroin, but never shot up.

My first intravenous experience with smack was brought about because of dope sickness. Others had told me that shooting would give faster relief than snorting, so I decided now was the time to shoot. I asked my friend, Brian, if he could fix me up. At first Brian thought I was joking because he knew I was afraid of needles. Brian also knew the ropes and could tell when an addict was in distress. I told him, "Fuck it. Hit me!" The tone of my voice and the look in my dope-sick eyes told Brian I was now ready to mainline. From that point on, I was hooked.

During the sixth hour of my Emergency Room care, the saline flush started to take effect. My electrolytes readjusted, and my blood chemistry became nontoxic. I reconnected with life through my ears first as I heard the steel whispers of my room curtain being whisked across the top rod. My eyes opened.

Dimly, I could see three silhouettes standing near my bed; Dad, Uncle Dan, and Mom. Mom arrived just as I regained consciousness. Dad had tried to phone her while he was on his way to the hospital to let her know what happened, but she wasn't available to answer the phone. When Mom got home, she picked up the message and came directly to the hospital.

Mom approached my bed while the twin brothers stood back and drew the curtain to allow her a private moment with me. I couldn't hear exactly what she was saying because she was crying, but I think Mom was telling me she loved me. I loved her too, however, I was in no condition to tell her. The three-quarter-inch plastic tube in my throat blocked my voice. Velcro restraints prevented me from reaching out my hand to signal that I loved her by touching.

After a few minutes, Mom stepped back so Dad and Uncle Dan could come to my bedside. Dad had a soft smile on his face. He leaned down to where I could feel his breath on my cheek and whispered, "I love you, Adam." just like he did when I was a little boy. He told me to get some rest, then he kissed my forehead and backed up. Uncle Dan kissed my forehead too but didn't say anything.

After two days, my young body rebounded, and I was ready to leave the hospital. As a condition of discharge, the RN asked if I had a place to live. I lied, telling her I planned to live at home with my dad. I knew Dad wouldn't permit me to come home, but the nurse didn't know this. If she had known that I had nowhere to live, she would have delayed my discharge until a social service professional was called in to feed me bullshit about staying at the Salvation Army or the Helping Hand Center.

What the RN didn't know was that I had visited the Salvation Army approximately eight months ago, after Dad kicked me out. I promised myself then that I would never again lay my body on a Salvation Army cot. My dignity would not be so easily surrendered. No matter how desperate my situation might become, I would rather die in the street than spend a night at the Salvation Army. As a fall-back, I was prepared to sleep in my Ford Explorer if Dad gave me the boot. In the past, I had lived out of my car, and I was ready to live out of my car again.

Even the strongest of the strong has a breaking point. There was little doubt I had taken Dad beyond his. Time after time I had betrayed his trust and disappointed him. Dad would be forced to protect himself. He would probably respond to my overdose by kicking me out of the house. This would be the fourth time in three years that I got the heave-ho. I braced myself for another of his "No goddamned doper will live in my house" routines. After his "instant replay" tirade, I would be granted 30 minutes to pack my bag, load my Explorer, and drive off to "I don't give a goddamn where you end up."

Dad met me at noon at the bottom of the hospital circle to take me home. I asked if he told Grandma that I overdosed, knowing that, of course, he had talked to her. He told me Grandma said I would have been better off if I had died, because I was in so much torment for so long that death was the only way for me to find peace. Grandma said I had no life, and my death would be a relief for everybody in the family. She was particularly worried about her own son and wondered how many more of my problems Dad could endure before he snapped.

It is hard to believe that Grandma would put a death wish on me. Out of 18 grandchildren, Ben and I were her hands-down favorites. She didn't want me to die – certainly not. Grandma's words were words of love, spoken at a time of stress. It was painful for her to see me living with so much helplessness and misery. In this context, I understood why she told Dad I would be better off dead. What I didn't know at the time was that Grandma kept votive candles burning for me in St. Anne's Shrine. A few dollars when she could afford it paid for the candles and helped Grandma maintain a spiritual connection with her own Higher Power. Grandma lived on a Social Security check. Prayers were free. Grandma said plenty of prayers for me – and plenty for Dad.

On the drive home I thought about telling Dad the truth – that I honestly never, ever would use dope again – but I didn't want to look like I was begging for a place to stay. After all, I was a tough guy, and groveling wasn't part of my character.

As soon as we entered our home, Dad asked me to sit with him at our kitchen table. This could only mean we were going to discuss terms and conditions of my departure. I gulped down a sudden burst of nausea and wondered whether Grandma was right. Probably I would be better off dead. I had no job, no friends, no education, and I had repeatedly betrayed the trust of my family. Soon I would have no place to live.

I watched as Dad set his jaw. He was preparing to deliver the knock-out punch. All my hopes of resuming a normal life with Dad and Ben would soon be dashed. With a cup of hot tea in his hand, Dad began by saying he had been thinking about the events that just took place. I thought, "Here it comes." Hopefully, my father would be merciful and just tell me to get the hell out. That scenario would be easier on me by far than listening to him go through that involved reasoning process of his, like he was arguing a case in court.

He began by explaining that sometimes in life bad things happen, not bad things MIGHT happen, but bad things WILL happen. When they do, the only question is: How can we take something bad and turn it into something good? He asked if I had any ideas about how to do this, but I knew his question was purely rhetorical. Dad said his first instinct was to throw me out of the house again, but if he did, my chance of survival would be nil. He had tossed me out before and nothing good resulted. On the other hand, if I were permitted to live at home and reflect upon my near-death experience, then perhaps I could build from it. Overdosing was a bad thing, no doubt. Learning from it would be a good thing. Besides, Dad didn't want to bring more pain into my already wretched life.

We sat and talked a half hour longer. I still had difficulty believing I was getting another chance to live at home. We planned to go slow, deal with problems as they arose, but make steady progress toward finding a life for me. Dad looked straight at me and said, "Adam, God must have a special plan for you, otherwise you wouldn't be here today.

If He hasn't given up on you yet, neither will we."

Two thoughts came to mind after Dad said this. First, if God has a special plan for me, then He must have a special plan for everybody, otherwise no one would be here. That assumes, of course, that God plans everybody's lives. The second thought was that if God truly has a special plan for me, then He let me come awful close to aborting the mission. Unless God's plan was that I should die so young. Which I hoped it wasn't.

Getting ready for bed that night, I stood before the big mirror behind the double bowl sink in the bathroom and took off my shirt. Holy shit! My body was black and blue from both elbows to my neck, across the shoulders, down the length of my chest to my waistline. I walked down the stairs to the kitchen to show Dad. I asked, "How did I get so banged up?" Dad replied that the bruises occurred while he was dancing me around the room, hoping to get my heart started. Then, seizing a chance to lighten the moment, Dad told me that after all the grief I had put him through, he ought to kick my ass again, right now! A faint smile crossed his face.

CHAPTER FOUR
Back to Normal

For Ben and me, breakfast was an important part of our family life growing up. Early morning was the one time we could all be together to eat. Dad believed that breaking bread bonds families, and therefore, eating together should be sacred. He explained that our ancestors survived by hunting and eating in groups, and this primitive tribal instinct carried itself to the present through rituals, which we know as mealtime. Sometimes, my dad had weird ideas. Which Ben agrees with me on this point.

I must admit, Dad prepared healthy cooked breakfasts for us boys. Drugging suppressed my appetite to the extent that a few bites of whatever Dad prepared in the morning was often the only wholesome food I would eat all day. I must also admit that as a family we did a lot of talking and stayed current with each other's lives at the breakfast table.

My brother wasn't home to greet me upon my return from the hospital following the heroin overdose. In February, 2003, he was manning a machine gun at an airbase in Riyadh, Saudi Arabia. Ben's college education was interrupted when his National Guard Unit, the 28th Military Police Company, was activated and deployed to the Middle East.

My dad and Uncle Dan are both Army veterans. They had gone through basic training together at Fort Indiantown Gap, Pennsylvania, and often reminisced about their military experiences. They encouraged Ben and me to sign up by bombarding us with cliches like, "It's something every man should do." Or another favorite, "You'll never regret it." Uncle Dan had three sons who served in the Marine Corps and one son currently serving in the Army. All four of his boys who went through college were able to finance their educations in part through various military assistance programs. Faced with this kind of background "encouragement" from his father and his uncle, what choice did 17-year-old Benjamin have but to enlist?

He joined the local National Guard Unit while still in high school and left for basic training one month after graduation. When Ben arrived at Ft. Leonard Wood, Missouri, the fact that he didn't need to shave yet made no difference to the Drill Instructors. To them, baby-faced Ben was just another raw recruit who didn't know jack shit. Under the D.I.'s gentle guidance, Ben would complete the journey from boy to man on the double quick. He would learn to stretch the skin across his ass just as tight as the next guy.

Ben adapted nicely to the early morning two-mile runs, the mirror-shined shoes, the K rations. He learned he could get along just fine on only four to six hours of sleep a day. Dad and I wondered how he was doing at Army camp. One day we got a postcard from Ben. It read, "Dear Dad, I have three weeks of basic training under my belt. It's not as much fun as you said it would be. Love, Ben." Dad laughed when he read the postcard, but I was genuinely concerned about my brother. "Don't worry about your brother," Dad reassured me, "When he comes home, he'll be a man."

At 18 or 19 years of age, a window opened where I would have been receptive to the adventure offered by a stint in the military. I talked to the Army and the Navy recruiters, but both refused to take me because of my seizure disorder and my brain tumor, even though I wasn't having problems with either.

With Ben away, just Dad and I posted for mess the next morning. Dad wanted our routine to return to normal as soon as possible. He avoided discussing my overdose incident, except to say that I should let my body rebound before trying to work on the basement project. It would be good for me to take a couple of days and just lay around the house doing nothing, and that's exactly what I planned to do – nothing. Dad left for his office with the understanding that life would be back to normal in no time. He was right.

Just before 11 o'clock, the phone rang. I answered.

"Hey, man, heard you went over the top the other day. What's with that, man?"

"Yeah, I dunno. Musta got some bad shit."

"Bad shit is right. You got into some pure 'snow,' man. That shit put you where you won't come back."

I hesitated. Part of me wanted to end the conversation on the spot. Part wanted it to continue. The conversation continued.

"Wanna do something?" asked my friend, Tony.

"Sure, why not?" I replied. This time, without hesitation.

"Cool. See you at my place in about forty-five."

Each day for the next five days, I drove to Tony's, and got a "wake up." Each day I felt the warmth of heroin spreading throughout my body. Each day I survived until the next. Things were back to normal. Just what Dad wanted.

On Saturday, in the middle of the night, Dad received a phone call from Saudi Arabia. It was Ben! The distance between Riyadh and Johnstown, Pennsylvania, spans nine time zones and Ben phoned without considering what time his call would be received back home. Talking over such distance presented a disconcerting one and a half second sound delay which produced some overtalking that took getting used to. Nevertheless, Dad and Ben enjoyed a 15-minute chat. As the conversation ended, Ben told Dad, almost as an afterthought, that he had not yet received his guitar. My father was dismayed to hear this, thinking I had mailed it to Ben ten weeks earlier.

I learned about the phone call the next morning at breakfast when Dad told me that Ben called. I asked how Ben was doing, and I told my dad how much I missed my brother. Of course, this was another of my big fat lies.

Living with my father all my life taught me to read him pretty accurately. Something ominous was brewing. The placid tone of Dad's voice confirmed, in my mind, that an eruption was imminent. "Adam, if you mailed Ben's guitar, say two months ago, don't you think he would have it by now?

Do you think overseas shipping is that slow, or, could it be you forgot to mail the guitar?"

Before I could blink, I was slammed against the doorway leading into the TV room, my back being bisected by the sharp edge of the oak trim. In one swift motion, Dad pinned me to the wall with a forearm shiver, crushing my windpipe. The pointing finger of his free hand was resting on my nose. I was gasping for breath! "You goddamned, worthless, useless, no-good piece of shit scumbag! I should tear your goddamned head off your shoulders! You little goddamned punk!"

Dad's right arm drew back, his fist clenched. He held it two feet away from my face, his eyes glazed with rage. My own eyes pleaded for mercy as I waited for my dad to finish me off by rearranging my face against the immovable door frame. I was totally defenseless. Ten seconds later, his grip on my neck loosened and his arm uncocked. He walked outside, brushing both hands through his thinning hair. Once again, I had cheated death.

Three months before I went to jail, Dad gave me $60 to mail a new acoustic guitar that he had purchased for Ben as a birthday present. I took the brand spanking new $460 guitar to Hi-Way Electronics where I hocked it for $150. I also pocketed the $60 postage money. Given Dad's volatile condition, I did not dare tell him that I also sold Ben's green electric Stratocaster guitar and floor amp at Hi-Way Electronics. The Stratocaster and amp together fetched $175, not really a good price considering that the Stratocaster alone cost over a grand.

One other thing I could never tell Dad was that I had

ransacked Ben's car after he went overseas. Ben was proud of his souped up Mazda MX-3 5-speed. Before shipping out, Ben parked the car in Pap's garage, winterized it, and covered it with blankets to keep it clean. I had no trouble at all removing the two 12-inch sub-woofers, the 600 watt amplifier, and the Sony CD player. Confessions! Now was not the time.

A few minutes later, Dad reentered the house. He commanded me to sit down at the table. Visions of packing my suitcase again appeared in my mind's eye.

Instead of continuing his tirade, Dad said he had thought things through. Selling Ben's guitar and stealing the shipping money occurred ten weeks ago, in the past. We needed to live in the present and move forward. Neither of us had the emotional stamina to continue revisiting unpleasant events which were irreversible. We had enough pressing matters on our plate at present. No sense impeding the path to progress with dead wood. Dad said under different circumstances, perhaps he would have given me the boot. For now, the best choice for both of us was to move beyond the guitar incident.

Later that day, Dad stopped at Wilson's Music Store and bought Ben another guitar, better than the one I sold. He shipped it himself that afternoon.

We lived in a two-story house. The second floor had three bedrooms of almost equal size. If you consider my dad as a boy, each boy had his own room. Ben's had a rust-colored carpet, Dad's carpet was dark blue, and mine was lettuce green. The very thought of having a lettuce-colored rug in my bedroom struck a blow to my manhood. I was a doper, yes, but also macho. Lettuce was a tad feminine for my taste. I covered the sissy green with a manly blue and yellow hand-braided heirloom rug that my grandma made and gave to me four years ago.

My bedroom was my sanctuary. When the door was closed, neither Dad nor Ben braved entry without first knocking and announcing, "Adam, can I come in?" or "Adam, we'll be late if you don't get moving." My lawyer father told us that we had a fundamental right "to be secure in our persons, houses, papers, and effects." Dad imposed a duty on each of us to respect the other's "right of privacy." When I put a personal item in one of my dresser drawers, I enjoyed an expectation that the drawer would not be opened without my permission, even in my absence. To my knowledge, Ben never violated my privacy; neither did Dad.

Dad told Ben and me that he, as parental "sovereign," reserved the right of "police authority" over the entire premises, including our rooms, but that he would exercise that authority only upon "probable cause." Dad always seemed to express his house rules in some bullshit legal jargon. This right of privacy thing was just one example.

On the other hand, the "right of privacy" was "waived" if the item were left out where it could be seen from the hallway. Dad called this the "plain view doctrine." I learned how the "plain view doctrine" applied when I was 13 years old. I stole a dirty magazine, "Elle," and left it lying on my dresser, open to a page featuring the "girl of the month." Dad noticed the magazine as he walked by the doorway and seized this contraband article, declaring that I had just been introduced to the "forfeiture doctrine." A couple days later, I saw "Elle" lying on Dad's night stand in "plain view," but I made no attempt to reclaim my property, even though turnabout would have been fair play. As parent, Dad was king, and over the years I also learned the legal principle that "the king can do no wrong."

I kept my stash in the bottom right-hand dresser drawer, a place I knew Dad never checked. Not once in all my years at home had he ever tossed my room. That gave me a measure of comfort. The housekeeper, Sandy, was more likely to find my weed than Dad. When Sandy cleaned, she had to organize my room and put my clean laundry back in the drawers. Sandy wasn't the type of person who would look through my bottom drawer just to see what she could find. Even if she found weed, I doubt that she would have told on me. I seldom stored heroin in the house, but once in a while, I would keep my works in the bottom drawer overnight.

Ben departed for military duty with the understanding that his room would be undisturbed. My brother didn't know that the very day his M.P. unit left town for overseas, I rummaged through his drawers looking for money. I found none, but I had struck the mother lode! Ben's checkbook and his expired photo I.D. drivers' license were lying right on top of his socks. It was now my turn to apply the "forfeiture doctrine." With checkbook in hand, "possession was ninety percent of the law." Oh, how I loved these legal principles!

On Sunday, we went to 9 o'clock Mass at St. John's Cathedral. I quit going to mass after I reached age 18. Church was a bunch of bullshit. Never did me any good. My dad agreed that a lot of it was bullshit. Still on most Sundays he attended Mass, and whenever I lived at home there was a rule that we go to church as a family. That's one of the few rules I respected; I'm not sure why.

During our talks, Dad reminded me that everybody needs a spiritual connection, since we are more than just physical beings. He wasn't all that concerned that I should embrace every tenet of the faith. Hell, I don't think he did. Dad wanted me to have a spiritual ground root that anchored me when the winds of temptation blew. He said nobody fighting addiction ever came through it without acknowledging something greater than mortal man. I think Dad was referring to what the twelve steppers call a "Higher Power." Survival was difficult enough while living on the edge. How could I be expected to develop sound spiritual values?

While I went through the motions of going to church, it did not change my mind set. There was me, numero uno, and in second place was the rest of the world. I could not have cared less for other people. For that matter, I didn't care much about myself. I constantly craved dope. If I prayed at all, it was for dope and money to buy dope. Dad's encouragement to seek God's help in my battle against addiction was an utter waste of his time, like an empty gong.

There was only one period of time in my life that I enjoyed going to church. That was when Ben and I were 11 or 12 years old. To make attendance at Mass fun for us, Dad would let us drive his car from home all the way to the church, a distance of more than five miles. Since ninety percent of the trip was by way of an empty four lane divided highway, the probability of a mishap was near zero. We each drove one way. If Ben drove to church, I drove home. If I drove in, he drove out. I don't mean Dad would sit us on his lap and let us steer the car. No, Dad moved to the passenger side and let us pilot his three-ton Lincoln Town Car from the time we put the keys in the ignition to the time we tuned the engine off and handed the keys back to him. We eagerly looked forward to our weekly driver's training classes. After Mass, we usually stopped for breakfast at the Donut Connection, across the street from the Cathedral.

By the second week home from the hospital, I think Dad was aware I had picked up again. Indicators abounded. I did very little work on the family room project. Free time was spent out with friends. My body weight dropped 20 pounds or more, and I was becoming increasingly impatient and irritable.

When Dad came home from the office, he would go directly to the family room and immerse himself in the remodeling project. Probably he did this work as a form of escape therapy. On Wednesday, Dad needed to drill a 5/8" hole into the block wall in order to set a tapcon anchor. He looked for his hammer drill, but couldn't find it. He was sure he had put it in the garage on a box near his tool chest. The garage was a disaster area because of the ongoing work, and therefore, Dad thought perhaps it was buried among the rubble. He spent one hour moving boxes and looking under empty containers and scrap piles, but still no drill.

Dad was as frustrated as I had ever seen him. "Now, Adam, that's a brand new DeWalt 18 amp hammer drill that I used yesterday. It didn't just walk away. That drill cost over $300. It has to be somewhere. Let's look again." For a few more minutes I helped Dad in his futile search for the power tool. Exasperated and exhausted, Dad unhitched his tool belt, tossed it onto the pile of scrap, and walked away talking to himself.

Earlier that day, my friends at Hi-Way Electronics had given $40 for the drill. Forty dollars. Enough to make me "right."

All during the next week my behavior became more daring. My physical appearance declined noticeably. I was back to using "H"– as many packs as I could steal the money to buy. Daily, I scoured the house for loose cash so I could buy more dope. If I couldn't find money, I would steal anything in the house that wasn't nailed down. Before construction began, Dad had boxed our collection of VCR movies and set them out of the way. I found the movies in the storage room and sold them outright to a friend, 20 movies for $75.

After Dad had "misplaced" the drill, he must have become suspicious of me because he no longer put his wallet on the microwave oven. One night I was so sick and desperate with withdrawal that I walked into Dad's bedroom while he was sleeping to see if his wallet was lying on the dresser, where he usually puts it. Talk about brass balls! Still, no luck.

When Dad came home from the office on Thursday, I wasn't there; neither was the television, the VCR player, Bose radio, clock radio from Dad's night stand, and our old stereo component system complete with speakers, amplifier, tape player, tuner, and recorder. All this property had found a new home at Hi-Way Electronics, under my signature, for the princely sum of $250. Only one thought crossed my mind as I was lifting father's goods into my Ford Explorer – doing this will help me get dope. I hardly remember pulling off the heist. When you are dope-sick and need a fix, consequences be damned! Two hundred fifty dollars would buy me enough heroin to get through a couple days.

Strangely enough, I returned home at approximately 10:30 that same night. I'm not sure why I went home, I guess I had no place else to stay. At the time, I was feeling smooth and confident. Whatever punishment Dad decided to hand down would be better than being strung out on dope. For sure, I was no match physically. I figured if Dad went nuts on me, he could kill me should he choose, and that would be just fine with me.

After I walked in the house, Dad came down the stairs and met me in the foyer. I braced myself for his bullrush. It didn't come. Meekly, my father looked at me and said, "Adam, for the life of me I wish I could think of a way to help you." He paused, then continued, "When this nightmare is over, I must answer the question: 'David, did you do everything in your power to help your son?'" Dad paused, then muttered, "I hope I did, Adam. I truly hope I did."

I was instructed to get a shower and a good night's sleep, because in the morning I would be leaving. Dejected, Dad walked up the stairs, and a few moments later I heard his bedroom door close.

Next morning, I awakened to the smell of bacon. I didn't shower that night, but I did next morning. It was a long, soothing, soapy shower, as if I were trying to wash away yesterday. I got dressed and went downstairs. Dad already had coffee in my cup and eggs over with bacon on my plate. We sat at the table together and made small talk while Dad read the newspaper.

After breakfast, Dad washed the dishes while I poured myself a second cup of coffee, attempting to garner a few more precious minutes at home. When he finished with the dishes, Dad told me it was time to pack my bags and leave. I realized that he had to protect himself from me, but I tried once more, without sacrificing my pride, to explain why I hocked the TV and other things. I told Dad I had no choice, that I had no control over myself and that I was sorry. Dad replied in a sullen tone, "I know, Adam. I know."

While I was in my bedroom packing, Dad came upstairs to help. He handed me a new toothbrush and a small tube of toothpaste. He also gave me an extra package of blades for my Gillette Trak III razor and included a bottle of Advil for when my back hurt. I finished loading the blue LL Bean duffle bag and a smaller black leather carry-on bag. Reaching my arm under the strap, I slung them over my shoulders and walked downstairs.

Dad told me the Ford Explorer would stay in the garage because I was using it for drugging, not for work. He said I had time to call for a ride, if I had any friends who might want to pick me up from home. Instead of responding, I asked what I would do for money, and Dad said that was my problem, that he had enough problems of his own. He told me to work the other side of the street. I copped an attitude for a moment and snapped, "Yeah, you're just going to put me on the street. I'll kill myself. That's what I'll do."

Staying calm, Dad responded that it was I who had put myself on the street, not him. He said he hoped I wouldn't kill myself, but there was nothing he could do to stop me because it was impossible for him to be with me around the clock. Which was true.

I was reminded that I could get my Tegretol at the Rite Aid Pharmacy next to Dad's office downtown. For meals, I could eat at Johnnie's Restaurant. All I had to do was sign the slip, and Dad would take care of the bill later. Dad asked me to call if I ever needed anything that could help me in my struggle with drugs, but cautioned me not to call unless I sincerely wanted help. The last thing Dad told me was to pray and dream, and always remember that I was a special child of God.

As my hand reached the doorknob, I sat the bags on the floor and turned around. We hugged each other for an eternity. Then Dad told me he loved me and said I must leave. Which I did.

C H A P T E R   F I V E
Street Smart

Dad kicked me out in mid-March 2003 when it was still plenty blustery up on the hill where I lived, or should I say, formerly lived. As I walked away from home, the wind whistled around my red ski jacket, and the cold penetrated into my bone marrow giving me the shivers, since I had no body mass to generate heat. Our neighbor, Dr. Fred was walking out his driveway to get the morning newspaper when he saw me leaving the house with my bags packed. Fred's look gave him away; he knew Dad had kicked me out of the house again. This awkward moment was shielded with a, "Good morning, Adam." I disrespectfully ignored Dr. Fred and continued trudging away because I was pissed off.

Passing motorists barely noticed me as I wiped the snot off my nose with the back of my hand and plodded down the hill toward my friend Will's house in the Hickory Grove section of town. With those cumbersome bags over my shoulder, I must have looked like an ant struggling with an object five or six times larger than the ant itself.

I wasn't sure if Will would let me stay with him, but he was my best lead. Moreover, the walk to Will's was only two and a half miles from home, and all downhill. A few years ago my dad did some legal work for Will. I wasn't aware of the details, but I am certain it was a criminal case. Last fall, Dad's associate, David Raho, helped Will get his driving privileges restored. I was hoping this favorable history Will had with my dad's law office would make it tough for him to say "no" when I asked if I could bunk over for a night or two.

Will was an alcoholic and an occasional pot smoker. Three years ago he moved to Johnstown from his native California in order to be closer to his wife's parents. Soon after the couple relocated, Will's wife double-crossed him by shacking up with another guy, leaving Will to raise the kids by himself – the Bitch! After the split, Will thought about taking his boys, ages six, eight, and ten, to California, but his California family had disowned him because of his heavy drinking. With no child support coming from his unemployed estranged wife, Will was hard pressed to provide even a meager living, working as a waiter by night and a handyman by day.

Heading up Maple Avenue, I recognized Will's clapped-out Ford Taurus parked on the street in front of the house he rented. All morning I had been toting half my body weight in two bags slung across my neck. My ass was dragging, and I was having a nicotine fit.

I turned in the walkway to the old frame house and tripped on an uneven cement slab. I fell, but didn't get hurt. The bags stayed on the ground. I got up and approached the front door. Thirty coats of grey paint over the old doorbell button made certain it would not work. I pressed the button anyway and waited for a chime. Nothing rang, so I put my eye up close to the beveled glass and took a peek. No signs of life on the inside. Will must be working. Shit!

I walked around back and stowed my bags on the porch out of sight, figuring to come back for them later. Suddenly, the back door opened part way. Will shouted through the crease, "Adam, what the hell are you doing here?"

"I need a little help. My dad kicked me out, and I don't have any place to stay. Just for a night. That's all I need."

Will invited me into the house and offered me coffee and a cigarette. I explained my circumstances over that cup of coffee. Will told me he has walked many miles in my moccasins, and he understood my predicament. Just the same, there was NO WAY he was letting me stay with him and his kids, not even for a night! He told me Attorney Weaver would understand. At that point I asked if he could lend me a couple bucks. He handed me a $20 bill.

Twenty dollars wasn't enough for dope, Will understood that. But it was plenty for food, cigarettes, or coffee at the nearby Sheetz convenience store. Nevertheless, Will was street-smart like me and knew that I would not spend money on cigarettes and coffee. An addict will spend every cent he has on dope. He knew I would steal cigarettes and get by without coffee. As for food, cash was too valuable to be wasted on crackers and hot dogs.

I understood why Will couldn't let me stay with him. His children were his priority, and he was barely making it. He didn't need an uninvited burden. Even swamped with problems, Will gave me what he could, thinking perhaps this gesture of kindness would lessen my misery, if only a little.

Nightfall came too soon; I still had no place to sleep. I made a few phone calls from the Sheetz payphone, but my dealer friends wouldn't answer a number that showed on their screen that they did not recognize. I worked my way back to Will's and waited in the alley until I saw his lights turn out. Then I sneaked up his rickety wooden back porch steps and bedded down in a corner away from the wind. I rolled myself in the muddy carpet runner and rested my head against the leather carry-on bag. A long frigid night would pass without any shuteye.

While I was looking for a place to stay, my dad was looking for his missing household items. Dad had only a faint idea where to start looking for his equipment, and he kicked himself for not asking me where I had fenced the goods. Pennsylvania laws ban pawn shops, nevertheless Dad suspected there must be an underground market for stolen property somewhere in the area. I could not have sold all that equipment to my friends, he reasoned.

As Dad drove down Hilltop Avenue with his girlfriend, Lisa, in the direction of his office, a radio spot came over the air advertising discount prices on all types of used electronic merchandise. The ad sponsor was Hi-Way Electronics. BINGO! The mystery was solved! Of course, I had unloaded the goods at Hi-Way Electronics. What's more, Hi-Way Electronics is located on Hilltop Avenue and was only a quarter mile down the road from where Dad heard the radio ad.

Dad and Lisa barged into Hi-Way Electronics. It didn't take long for Lisa to spot several of the stolen objects, including the VCR player, which was hers. She brought it to our house several months earlier so she and Dad could watch movies. It became a household fixture. The 17" Sharp model TV was nestled among twelve or fifteen other televisions that all looked the same to Dad. This camouflage was not effective against Lisa, however, and she singled out that TV as if it were the spotted zebra in a herd.

It was the 17-inch Sharp TV and Dad's new Bose Sound Wave radio which concerned him most. Dad didn't care if he ever recovered his digital clock radio that he kept on the nightstand. There were too many buttons for him to figure out how to set the alarm. Dad got the times all screwed up. Sometimes the alarm would go off in the middle of the night, and I'd hear Dad over in his room cursing "the sadistic bastard who designed this goddamned thing!"

The older stereo stack system with two big speakers stood in the corner with a For Sale tag offering it at $500. This one Dad recognized immediately as his old system. The day he unboxed it and assembled the cabinet I swung from the door and sprung the hinge. Now the door latched only by lifting it into position and pushing . To be sure, Dad opened the door. It was sprung! What better proof of ownership could there be?

My dad spoke to the attendant at the counter, a man in his mid-20's. He told the man that he had come to recover his stolen electronic equipment. Whereupon the young man went to a back office and returned with the manager, a fellow around Dad's age. His name was Chuck. Coincidentally, forty odd years ago Dad and Chuck grew up in the same neighborhood, one block apart, at a time when neighbors knew each other.

Dad explained the circumstances to Chuck, expecting Chuck to allow him to reclaim his goods hassle-free. It didn't go down that way. Chuck pulled two slips from his records bearing my signature, showing he paid me $275 for everything. Chuck wanted reimbursed. My dad saw the issue differently.

"There is no way I'm paying you for something I already own."

"Well unless you redeem this merchandise for what I paid your son, the stuff doesn't leave the store." Chuck fired back.

Dad was already primed to explode when he walked into the store. The thought of a kid who was strung out on drugs being able to cart an armload of electronic gear into a store and walk out with a handful of money left no doubt about the character of the store owner. It was disappointing that Chuck seemed to have lost his moral bearing, particularly in a transaction involving an old neighborhood buddy. There was a time when Chuck and my father shared the same playground, shot hoops on the same basketball court, and even chased after the same girl, Snookie. Neither Dad nor Chuck had exclusive rights to Snookie. She was a playground favorite.

Both men were getting testy. Not even Snookie could have pacified them. Dad's next statement had an edge on it.

"Chuck, perhaps you didn't hear me. I said I'm not

paying you for something I already own."

Chuck's reply had an equally sharp edge. "Dave, perhaps you didn't hear me. Unless you pay, the stuff doesn't leave the store."

Chest to chest, chin to chin, Chuck and Dad stood, each waiting for the other to budge. As if on cue, the Hilltop Borough cop, Sergeant Tom Dixon, hurried into the store and separated Chuck and Dad. Sensing trouble earlier, the younger fellow behind the counter had placed a call.

Both Chuck and Dad respected Sergeant Dixon's police authority and settled themselves long enough to tell their stories. After hearing both sides, Sergeant Dixon told Dad he would have to pay Chuck in order to reclaim the goods.

Dad cut loose with a diatribe, telling the cop he wouldn't pay a penny to a goddamned fence. Chuck was a complicit middle man who made it possible for addicts like his son to buy dope. Furthermore, Chuck should be arrested for the crime of receiving stolen property as well as the crime of conspiring to distribute drugs. Dad told Sergeant Dixon to arrest the son-of-a bitch on the spot. Which he should have.

"Come on, Dave, you know I can't arrest Chuck? He has the slips to show the transaction is legal."

"He is trying to cover his crooked ass with a sales slip. They're just as bogus as the rest of this store. Eighty percent of the stuff in here is stolen. Just look around."

Dad pressed on, telling Sergeant Dixon that sales slips only go to prove Chuck's involvement. He explained the elements of the crime of Receiving Stolen Property and told

Sergeant Dixon that in order to make a case against Chuck, it was not necessary to prove that Chuck actually knew the goods had been stolen, only that Chuck believed that the property had PROBABLY been stolen. This point of law did not change Dixon's mind.

Hearing this, Chuck lashed back at my dad, telling him that if he had done his job as a father, his son would not have grown up to be an addict. Now, Attorney Weaver was trying to blame everybody but himself for a problem kid that he created because of negligent parenting.

Furious, my father's face flushed. The presence of the police officer allowed Chuck to keep his teeth and retain the shape of his head. Exercising all his powers of restraint, Dad pivoted away from Chuck, picked up his Sharp TV, and began carrying it toward the door.

"Put it down, Dave, or I'll have to arrest you." Dixon commanded, with an emphasis on "you."

As he walked out the door still hefting the TV, Dad looked over his shoulder at the Sergeant, "That's right, Tom. You'll have to arrest me."

Loading the TV in his car must have taken some fight out of my dad, because he came back in the store in a more conciliatory mood. Tightening his neck, he asked Chuck if the Sony stereo system would bring enough to cover his out of pocket costs, and, if so, Chuck could keep the stereo.

This settlement proposal might work because it allowed both men to save face. Chuck would retain enough electronic equipment to recover the money he paid to me, and my father would get back the goods he wanted without reaching in his pocket for cash.

Chuck nodded his acceptance to those terms. Dad loaded his car with the rest of his equipment. Lisa strutted out of Hi-Way Electronics, brandishing her VCR and swaying her ass left and right to send a message of her own to Chuck.

By 6 a.m. the next morning, I shivered and smoked my way to the Sheetz store for a hot coffee. For breakfast, I stole a Snickers bar. I was starting to feel sick again from not having dope in my system, and I hoped the Snickers would provide enough of a sugar rush to forestall severe symptoms until I scored. My chances of running into someone who was holding were good, if I just hung around long enough. The only problem was, I didn't have much money. But I had a plan. When I needed money for dope, I always had a plan.

Around 9:30, two teen aged punks stopped for gas and came into the store after they topped off the tank. Their baggy pants and oversized shirts labeled these losers as users, probably just getting into it. The smaller blond kid had a ring in his ear and a stud in his nose. I felt safe about approaching them both. Most likely, these two dummies had a supplier for all the pot they could smoke, so there was no sense in me trying to hustle marijuana. To scam these boys, I needed something different.

I walked over to the dominant boy and asked if he ever did "schrooms" and whether he wanted to try them. He said "no" to both questions; but to my surprise, the blond haired passenger spoke up, saying he heard they were "cool." I told them I recently got some of the best I ever had and I could get more from an undisclosed source. I explained that my dealer wouldn't sell in quantities under an ounce and quoted them the street price of $200. They took the bait.

All three of us jumped into their white Jeep Grand Cherokee and motored up the hill to the Frankstown Shopping Center. Outside the Ideal Grocery Store, near the return station for shopping carts, was a wall mounted MAC machine. The dumb blond fed his plastic into the machine, pushed a few buttons, and the machine regurgitated money.

Two hundred dollars later, we were headed down the hill, following my directions to the source's location. My friends understood it was necessary for us to park a little distance away from the dealer and that I would need to go alone. Since the seller could not identify them, they had to remain out of sight because their presence might quash the deal. Furthermore, the boys understood that I needed to take an indirect route as a precaution against detection by suspicious neighbors, who might alert the police to the dealer's location.

The deal that was going down had been presented to the two young marks in such a way as to create an element of intrigue, if not charm. I could tell they were thrilled to be players. I had informed the boys that the entire transaction should take only five or ten minutes, and they should wait in the Jeep for me to return, probably by a different route. Off I sneaked with the dope money, walking through the backyards and between houses while my gullible friends waited in the Jeep, and waited, and waited.

It might seem easy to beat a couple of rookie drug users out of $200. In a sense it was easy, but in another way it was hard, far too hard. Being an addict with no job is the hardest job anyone could ever have. When you're an addict, every waking moment and half your sleeping moments are occupied by just one thought – how can I get money for dope. Worrying about paying for your next high dominates all your time and saps all your energy. Selfishness rules. Moms and dads, brothers and sisters, girlfriends, best friends, are nobody. I stole money from my mom and dad every chance I could. When I didn't steal directly from them, I stole indirectly. I can't remember a single time they handed me money for legitimate purchases that I actually used the cash for its intended purpose.

No addict can survive without being good at lying, cheating, or stealing, and I was an accomplished professional at all of these. After I graduated from high school, I frequently had lunch with my mom. I would call her at work and ask if she wanted to meet me on her lunch break, and, of course, she was pleased that I called. Since I initiated the lunch date, she thought I actually wanted to see her. In truth, all I wanted was her money. I endured the lunch meetings hoping Mom would slip "poor Adam" a few bucks when we were finished eating. Which she usually did.

When I was growing up, I was plagued with self-doubt and very little self-esteem. Dad and Mom both recognized my lack of self-confidence, and both heaped praise on me for ordinary achievements. They tried every trick in the book to boost my ego. I remember Dad saying, "Adam, I need a real good pool shooter to be my partner. What do you say you and I give Uncle Dan and Ben a lesson?" Dad would even try to make me feel better about myself by directing my attention to people who truly were limited. He would tell me to just look around at all the doofuses in the world. Sometimes he would point a few out to me when we were riding in the car or walking in the mall. He would randomly select someone and say, "Look at that doofus, Adam." When I think about Dad comparing me to doofuses, I realize that he was comparing me with oddballs who were perhaps not a representative sample of the general population. Which doesn't make me feel too good. Being compared to a doofus wouldn't make anybody feel good. I don't care who you are.

Of course, Dad wasn't really making fun of other people so much as he was trying to demonstrate to me, in a concrete way, that I was as smart as the next guy. My mom was more subtle, but equally ineffective, in her efforts to inflate my ego.

Regardless of whether Dad and Mom were right, I was clever enough to beat two potheads out of $200. The best part of that score was that I walked away with cash, all twenties, and it was a low risk scam. I didn't need to forge checks, pass through exit sensors with stolen goods, or use false ID. The dummy just handed me the money. Nothing could be easier than that. Now, the question remained, "Was I smart enough to spend the money wisely?" Which I never was.

The smart approach would have been to assess my desperate situation and figure out how a couple hundred dollars might best be spent for necessary life support. If I were smart, I would have rented a cheap motel room so I could shower some of the stink off my body, brush my teeth, shave, and rejoin the human race.

Smart or not, reason yielded to a greater power. It had been a day and a half since my most recent fix. Now that I had money, an indescribable force got hold of me, driving me, directing me, and dominating me as if my very survival depended upon finding dope. Which it did. Instead of reserving a cheap motel room, I bummed a ride to the mall where I planned to meet a friend who deals.

Heroin had become my drug of choice, and it was heroin I needed to shake the nausea of early-onset withdrawal. The $200 I conned bought eight stamp bags and a rig. I walked out of the mall with my friend and sat in the cab of his black Chevy pickup truck where I cinched a brown leather belt tight around my upper arm. Ahhhh! Come warmth! Come! Spread throughout my body!

Night came and, once again, I was without money or a bed. Once again I would endure the cold temperatures and the onion snows in my dirty red ski jacket, oversized blue jeans, and Italian-made hiking boots. It didn't matter to me that I had blown all my money. My body needed dope a lot more than it needed a bed.

When the mall closed, my friend drove me down the hill to Hickory Grove. Earlier in the day, I stashed my bags in an abandoned garage located at the end of Collier Street near the Stonycreek River. For the next three nights, I would bivouac in this drafty dark rectangle just beyond the shadow cast from the last city street light.

C H A P T E R   S I X
Fireworks

It had been nearly a week since my last shower and my body was giving off an offensive odor even I could smell. My red ski jacket reeked of stale cigarette residue, and the nicotine coating on my throat was so thick it could be scraped off with a putty knife. At one time, my teeth were perfect and white. Now, they were tar-stained and full of cavities. Heroin destroys the decay fighting properties of saliva. Without this natural protection, my teeth began to rot. The new toothbrush Dad packed stayed in my bag alongside the bottle of multivitamins he also shoved in. An occasional Snickers bar I stole from Sheetz fed me, and cup after cup of coffee kept my battery charged. At age 21, I was slipping fast.

Fearing my emaciated body would lose all of its heat if I laid directly on the rough concrete floor, I spread old newspapers several rows thick for insulation and laid on the newspapers, trying to conform my angular body to a flat surface. Thanks to my near exhaustion, sleep did manage to get the upper hand on discomfort from time to time. Mostly,

I just jostled in a state of semi-awareness, my thoughts now and then peeping through clearings in the ever present dope fog.

During the second night of tossing and turning on the cold newspaper bed, a smile came across my face, brought on by pleasant childhood memories.

When we were 13, Dad and his girlfriend took Ben and me to the Bahamas for a mid-winter getaway. In anticipation of the trip, Dad got each of us snorkel gear from the L.L. Bean catalog. Without an ocean at home, I practiced snorkeling on a sea of blankets and pillows in my bedroom in order to be ready for the real thing.

The trip to the islands was also the first time Ben and I wore our contact lenses. As we were getting ready for our maiden dive, Dad made us go into the motel bathroom and try out our new contacts. We fumbled with contact fluid and eyelids for fifteen minutes, and neither of us could get the hang of it. Five or six times we came out of the bathroom with blood-shot eyes, but no contacts in. Each time, Dad sent us back to try again. Snorkel masks do not fit over eyeglasses. "Either learn how to wear contact lenses, or miss seeing the splendor of the underwater world." At last, we figured it out, and both of us proudly blinked our way down to the beach.

During our dives, Ben was afraid, so he stayed as close to Dad as a baby whale to its nursing mother, whereas I fearlessly ventured all over the Carribean Sea. I was born to dive.

Ben acquired three new talents on that vacation: he

learned to snorkel; he learned to put contacts in; and he learned to swear. At least, that was the first occasion I ever heard him swear. Ben swears pretty regularly now.

When we were 14, Ben and I got jobs bussing tables at Rizzo's Restaurant. Dad thought working would teach us the value of a dollar and give us a little responsibility. We filled out the state work permit applications by ourselves. After they were approved, we worked part time for the next two years and saved enough money for a down payment on our first car, a blue 1992 Pontiac Grand Am. There should have been more money, but I squandered a big chunk of my earnings on pot.

Between ages 13 and 16, Ben and I rode dirt bikes. Ben's was a yellow Suzuki which Dad bought from his friend, Randy. Mine was a red Honda purchased used from a dealer. As accessories for the dirt bikes, we had colorful riding clothes, high safety boots, elbow protection, padded pants, helmets and goggles – the works!

At our house we practiced the "different but equal" theory. Since Ben's bike was used, it wouldn't be right for me to get a brand new one. Throughout our lives, we got the same quality things, but a little different, whether it was baseball gloves, skis, golf clubs, or clothes.

On Saturdays, six or eight of our friends would round up in our backyard with their own dirt bikes, forming a posse. Off we would go with Hellman's mayonnaise jars full of gasoline tied to our seats in case we ran out of fuel. One of our favorite destinations was McNally Bridge. After a five-mile ride bouncing through woods and dashing across busy township roads, we arrived at the bridge. Often we climbed the steel superstructure past the "No Trespassing" signs and scaled out to the center of the steel arch, 250 feet above the Stonycreek River, which cuts a winding path along the valley floor.

In the winter time, Dad took Ben and me skiing every Wednesday. We were better skiers than Dad after our second outing. Soon Ben and I became experts, but not Dad. I enjoyed the cuts and jumps and speed of skiing and also the *apres ski*, which to me meant hot chocolate and sandwiches with Dad and his friend Randy in Randy's chalet.

My Dad has a family of friends who own the Seven Springs Ski Resort. Somehow, through these friends, we were annual guests at a little cabin right at the top of the main ski run overlooking the whole complex. We were given VIP treatment and enjoyed three or four days at the cabin year after year.

Chipmunk Lodge was a rustic one-story log structure finished with rough boards, except for the floor, which was sanded and varnished. There was a round fire pit in the middle of the cabin and a good supply of already split wood, stacked on a pile in a spillover mud room. At night when the fire was crackling, we would come in from skiing and hang our cold wet clothes along the fire's edge. Hot dogs over the fire and a cup of hot chocolate hit the spot. Pap and Grandma always enjoyed our ski weekend at Chipmunk. They would sit for hours at the window drinking coffee, playing cards, or just watching the skiers zig-zagging down the slopes.

Our hosts provided enough ski passes for everybody, including our cousins from Mom's side, Jeff and Steve. Not every adult could ski, but it was exciting for them to ride in the snow groomer all over the slopes. One year Ski Patrol professionals gave Pap and Grandma a special tour of the facilities by snowmobile. The excited look of children at Christmas came across their 80-year-old faces whenever the big sleds roared away from Chipmunk, as the oldsters clung to their drivers' goose down parkas.

On most Sundays, Mom took Ben and me to visit her folks. They lived on a farm, and there was always something fun to do on tap. My cousins, Jeff and Steve, liked sport shooting. Hour after hour we shot clay pigeons with shotguns, or stationary targets with rifles and pistols. We got so expert any of us could plunk a squirrel out of a tree with a .22 long from a hundred yards, or take the head off a groundhog with a high-powered rifle from 250 yards.

Another of our fun activities was driving the all-terrain vehicles across the fields and through the hemlock woods on the lower end of the farm. We often spent the whole day exploring along logging roads which crisscrossed through the forest.

There was an apple orchard on the farm with a variety of apples, including Northern Spy, Golden Delicious, Jonathan, Yellow Transparent, Red Delicious, and Wine Sap. Pappy Kuncelman kept the orchard pruned and sprayed, resulting in plentiful harvests of succulent fruit. In the fall, we squeezed apples through Pappy's cider press. Making cider was work then, but it is a happy memory now – as I dreamed it.

Every Sunday at noon, Grandma Kuncelman rang the dinner bell. Like trained dogs, we put down our guns or scooted home on our quads to take our place at the table for an old-fashioned country feed. Nobody could spread a table like Grandma Kuncelman.

These pleasant thoughts floated through my mind as I drifted in and out of sleep on the newspaper bed in the cold garage. Did God send such happy memories to protect me from being overwhelmed by my present circumstances? In my heart I still knew I was God's special child and that He had a plan for me. If only I could figure it out. I hoped I soon would. My pain was a pain maybe only God could understand – a pain only He could take away. So every now and then, just when I needed it, God carried me back to my childhood and let me live it again in my dreams.

We played a lot of ice hockey during the winter months when I was young. When we were seven or eight years old, Dad and Mom drove us to Pittsburgh to play an exhibition event with the National Hockey League Penguins at the Civic Arena. Ben and I actually skated a shift with Mario Lemieux, the greatest player of all time, but I doubt if Mario remembers skating with us.

For summer fun, nothing beat cottage life at Camp Sunshine. Uncle Ray and Aunt Lois had a cottage there, and so did Uncle Dan and Aunt Carol. Each cottage sat along the banks of Dunnings Creek and stood on posts four or five feet above ground level to protect against flooding. Camp Sunshine was the focal point for family activities. My cousins Alex and Lee are within six months of Ben and me in age. Kevin is two years older, and the other cousins never did grow up, so a few years difference in age meant nothing. Claire and

Elaine are the only girls in this dirty dozen. Still, they fit right in with the boys, Mark, Paul, Justin, Russ, Matt, Eric, Chris, and Patrick.

We played volleyball, horseshoes, and lawn croquet. We built bonfires and roasted corn in the hot coals. We swam in the muddy creek and fished for smallmouth bass and carp. We played a card game called Hoss and were ever-present kibitzers at the bridge games the adults played.

On the Fourth Of July, we put off a fireworks display that drew spectators from all over the camp. The campers brought lawn chairs and sat on the edge of the riverbank while we whizzed rockets and starbursts over their heads from the other side of the river. Kevin and I were the bravest at lighting fuses and scampering away before the flames started shooting. Next morning, we all worked together gathering duds and spent rocket tubes policing the area around ground zero.

Thinking about Camp Sunshine brought back one memory that wasn't so enjoyable. I was probably 15 or so when I stole $35 from the purse of a guest at Uncle Ray's cottage. I never admitted to the theft, and Aunt Lois did not directly accuse me, but I detected a tone in her voice during the questioning that told me she knew I was the thief. To this day, I never apologized.

By age 16, I was giving Dad nothing but A-T-T-I-T-U-D-E at home. Seemingly, little things came between us, like my longer hairstyle, my baggy pants, and my big shirts. I guess these weren't so little to Dad. "You look like a punk, Adam. You were raised better than that. When I get home, you'll have a haircut, or I'll cut your damn hair." I never let up on

Dad. Every one of his rules became the subject of my defiance, usually in the form of passive aggression, but sometimes with overt opposition.

For instance, Dad had a rule that there would be no hate music played in the house, and CDs containing hate music were not to be brought onto the premises. We were never given a clear definition of hate music. Dad said he'd know it when he heard it, but almost all rap fit Dad's definition. He said he didn't understand how white kids could enjoy listening to black racists "motherfuck" their way from one CD track to the next. "That shit can't be good for you."

Quite often, my friend, Ron, would bring his CDs to our house after school where we would shoot pool and listen to music before Dad got home. One day he came home early. We heard footsteps upstairs. We were playing rap, the kind he banned. This was my opportunity to test Dad's rap rule. I jacked up the volume until it boomed out of our family room and caused every wall in the basement to pulsate.

Predictably, my father swallowed the bait. He walked down the stairs to the family room, and without a word marched directly to the CD player and turned it off. Next, he confiscated about twenty of Ron's CDs and broke each one across his knee while Ron and I looked on. Then he found my case of CDs and busted about twenty more. The only one he didn't break was "The Best Of Patsy Cline," which was in my case by mistake.

This episode and others like it, provoked my father, out of frustration, to tell me I had a choice of living with him and Ben as civilized human beings, or if I continued my disrespectful, disruptive conduct, he would ship me to the county juvenile facility. Which I think he would have.

When we were juniors in high school, Dad planned a three day ski vacation to Taos, New Mexico. There were four in our party, Dad, Dave Raho, Ben, and me. Two days before we were scheduled to leave, I decided to quit school. I stayed in bed until Dad knocked on my door and entered to find out if I was sick. Smugly, I remarked that I had decided to quit school. My dad asked if I would care to enlighten him on how I planned to take care of myself, now that I had become emancipated. Of course, I had no sensible answer. He suggested I accompany him to his office where we would discuss the issue at greater length, but first we would stop to see Grandma and Pap, a morning routine for Dad.

When we walked into my grandparents' house, Grandma hurried across the kitchen to give me a hug and a kiss in her cheerful way. "Adam! How's my special boy today? What's the matter? No school?"

"Adam decided he doesn't need to go to school. He plans to drop out. We're going to my office and talk about it." said Dad, directing an obvious wink to Grandma and Pap and intoning his voice in that condescending, lawyer way of his that really pissed me off.

Pap didn't say much, but Grandma wouldn't shut up. On and on she went, lecturing me about the importance of an education. She asked three times whether I wanted to wash cars the rest of my life and stand in the unemployment line. "Is that what you want to do?" she badgered.

Derisively, I spit back an answer to Grandma, "I don't give a fuck what I do!"

Instantly, Dad was in my face. "Don't you ever talk to your grandma like that! You better show some respect, not only for her, but for yourself. Do you understand?"

Without thinking, I shoved my dad and cursed him, "Get your fuckin' hands off me!" At the same time, my right fist targeted my father's jaw. His peripheral vision provided warning enough to jerk his neck straight back and rotate his head to the right. My looping one hander only grazed.

One heartbeat later, I was staring at the ceiling and my head was resting against the kickplate on Grandma's kitchen cabinets. My dad was on top, using his body weight to subdue me. Dad simply pancaked me as if Grandma had flipped me from the griddle to the floor. Faintly I heard him say, "Settle down, Adam." But the fight wasn't yet over.

All things being equal, I was no match for my bigger, stronger father. But all things were not equal. Deep in my baggy pants pocket, I groped for the switchblade. It had a four-inch cutting surface and snapped open with an easy flick of the wrist. No sooner had the blade flashed, than Grandma shrieked, "Oh my God! He's got a knife!"

Faster than Grandma's panicked warning echoed off the cupboards, Dad clamped my wrist and muscled my arm to an outstretched position.

My pap, still contractor strong at 82, jumped into the mix. He kneeled on my forearm and pried open my fingers until the weapon fell to the linoleum. Pap picked up the knife, and my dad moved aside so I too could stand. There was no more commotion. No yelling or screaming. A calm settled in, as if my tormentor had been exorcized. Everyone intuitively sensed the danger had passed. Which it had.

My dad asked if I would tell him what was bothering me. Seventeen-year old boys do not normally foul-mouth their grandparents and pull knives on their dads. Dad said we were dealing with safety issues, mine and theirs. He directed Pap to place two phone calls; one to the Johnstown Police Department to dispatch a cruiser; and the second to Cambria County Mental Health Crisis Intervention Unit to dispatch a case worker.

Meanwhile, I waited in the sunroom for the police to arrive, brave on the outside, but scared to death on the inside. When you just got done pulling a knife on your dad and the cops are on the way, you're scared. Anyone would be scared in these circumstances. I don't care who you are.

First on the scene was patrolman Jerry Mesko of the Johnstown Police Department. Pap met the officer at the kitchen door and let him in without waiting for a knock. The policeman was wearing a heavy black belt, thicker than the one I wore when I was being transported to the Westmoreland County Jail. Attached to the belt were handcuffs, radio, flashlight, a big gun, and other items of police paraphernalia that I didn't recognize. Officer Mesko was an inch or two shorter than me in height, but his forearms were as thick as my legs.

My dad seemed pleased that Officer Mesko was the person dispatched to the scene. "Jerry, I'm sorry to drag you here, but I'm also glad you're the guy on duty."

"That's ok, Dave. What's up? Problems with your son, I guess?"

"Can we get you any breakfast, Jerry? At least a cup of coffee."

There I stood listening to small talk between my dad and the responding police officer, and thinking my new home will soon be the Juvenile Detention Center.

Dad spoke up, "Jerry, I think we should wait for Mental Health to get here and assess Adam. He has a history of severe depression and threatened self-harm. If he checks out all right, and there is no danger to himself or us, then we'll go from there."

Ten minutes later, a brown-haired woman came to the kitchen door. Pap greeted her and let her in. The woman displayed her credentials and introduced herself as Helen Backus. She spoke with the adults for a few minutes, then she consulted with me privately in the sunroom where I had been waiting.

Helen asked a lot of questions about my medical and drug use history. She wanted to know what prescription medicines I was taking. I told her I took Prozac for depression and Tegretol to guard against seizures. Helen asked if I used drugs, and I replied that I used marijuana occasionally. This was another big fat lie! Was this social worker so naive as to expect the truth from a hardcore druggie? I did not tell Helen about my heavy use history with LSD, cocaine, crystal meth, Ritalin, or any of the others. No sense disclosing more than was necessary. Just get through the interview session. This caseworker was writing notes as fast as her fingers could fly. I figured there would be another file set up which the county would use against me in Juvenile Court proceedings. What good would it do me to spill my guts?

We talked about my previous hospitalization when I was 13 for threatening to kill myself and my dad. She asked what I thought about school. I told her I hated school and wanted to quit. The lady said since I only had a year and a half left, wouldn't it be a good idea to stay until graduation? I didn't answer.

Next, Ms. Backus asked a lot of questions about why I pulled the knife. Did I intend to use it? Why was I packing a weapon as opposed to a pocket knife? Had I used it before to threaten anybody? Did I ever cut myself on purpose? Did I ever think about killing myself? Was I thinking about killing myself now? Was I planning to kill some other person?

After 30 minutes, the case worker rejoined the adults to discuss the results of her interview with me. She agreed that safety was the critical issue, and based on her discussions with me, she did not think I presented an immediate danger to myself or others.

At this point, Helen returned to the sunroom to inform me of her decision. She leveled with me, telling me she examined me to determine whether I had suicidal or homicidal inclinations. Ms. Backus reported that in her opinion, based upon the interview, I was not an immediate threat to myself or others. Therefore, she was not recommending placement in the County detention facility. However, since I had acted out in a manner that was very serious, Helen told me she would assist my father in arranging follow up counseling for me. In the meantime, Officer Mesko was going to retain the knife, for which Dad signed a receipt. A Police Incident Report would be on record, but no charges would be filed.

Shortly thereafter, everyone left Pap's house. Dad and I planned to go to his office to talk things out a little more. On the drive to the office, Dad reached his hand over and put it on my knee and asked if I was still shook up. I told him, "A little." Dad said I had to try to forget about what happened, but at the same time learn from it. Above all, Dad cautioned me not to think about what could have happened. "What if" analysis would serve only to create issues that don't exist. It's a mistake to start thinking about what if I had actually stabbed him; what if someone had been killed; what if I had gone to jail for life. None of these "what if" things happened, and therefore, I should not burden my mind trying to find solutions to problems that don't exist. There are enough real problems that do exist for us to worry about.

As we walked down the street for lunch at Johnnie's Restaurant, I said to Dad, "Well, it looks like I won't be going on any ski vacations to New Mexico with you and Ben on Friday."

My dad answered, "Adam, right now I can't think of anybody who needs a ski vacation more than you do."

Sure enough, we went on that ski vacation: me, Ben, Dave Raho and Dad, and for those three days, Ben and I skied like Olympic champions. I don't know how much good it did me to go, but I have a lot of happy memories of that ski trip.

Too bad life is more complicated than hot chocolate and fireworks, or corn roasts and card games. Why must the dark side so frequently overshadow pleasant dreams and happy memories? The answer to this question would have to wait. Life at present was a newspaper bed – nothing more.

CHAPTER SEVEN

Scams

Photo sensors had done their job and switched off the street lamp before I awoke next morning. The night had been unusually tranquil, no heavy winds or manmade noises. To the east, the sun was announcing its intention to pull more tulips out of the ground today. It was March 20, 2003, and it looked like spring would arrive one day ahead of schedule. A perfect day for drugging.

At 9 o'clock I phoned my mom from the Sheetz and asked if she could meet me for lunch. The hitch in her answer confirmed that she knew about me stealing Dad's TV and other stuff. Without waiting for Mom to question me about the theft, I came right out and told her that Dad gave me the boot two days ago. My pre-empt did not work. Mom pressed for more details. She asked where I was living. That question led into my hand. Begging off a precise answer, I said I had made arrangements to share an apartment with a friend, which was another reason I called her. My $200 portion of the first month's rent was due, and I needed a loan. Mom said she couldn't give me rent money because she believed I would use it to buy drugs. In my most pitiable voice, I implored Mom for financial help, reminding her how much it embarrassed me to ask for money. Hoping to push her sympathy button, I reported that I had been sleeping in the street.

"Adam, I feel terrible about your circumstances, but when you get money in your pocket, you blow it on drugs. I want to help you, you know I do, but I can't keep feeding you money. I just can't."

"I really need your help now, Mom. Just one month's rent. After that, I'll be able to pay my own way."

"Adam, who is this other person you're planning to share expenses with?"

This question was all the opening I needed. From here on, getting $200 from her would be easier than taking $200 from that dumb kid who thought he was buying hallucinogenic mushrooms. "His real name is Gordon, but everybody calls him 'Hoss,' and he lives in Eastmont. I'll bring Hoss along, and you can give the money directly to him."

Had I told Mom the truth, she would have known Hoss was my supplier of heroin. Hoss played along with the rent ruse I contrived in order to con Mom out of money for drugs.

At lunchtime, Hoss and I met Mom at the Eat-N-Park restaurant. Hoss told Mom he was a roofer and was hoping to get back to work when the weather broke. She bought the story. She also bought lunch, and with the $200 she handed Hoss, she bought ten packs of smack, seven for me and three for my big friend.

Part of that line of shit I fed my mom was true. I was

planning to share an apartment with Hoss, and I did move in with him, but only for a brief period of time. Big Hoss was on probation for selling drugs. His Probation Officer drug tested him two weeks ago, and Hoss had "hot" urine. What a surprise! A violation hearing was scheduled for March 27. Hoss knew for certain the Judge would rule he had violated Condition #3 of his probation, which commanded him to refrain from all drug use.

The thought of spending an additional thirty days in the slammer left Hoss feeling melancholy. We discussed the situation and agreed that if Hoss were to go to jail, I should use his black Chevy pickup truck and keep his users supplied until his release. In the meantime, I could serve as his apprentice and learn the business. Which I already mostly knew.

Almost all of Hoss' drug deals happened by appointment. A user would call his cell phone and set a meeting time and place, usually the mall parking lot. Since his conviction, Hoss had become skittish about dealing out of his apartment. Occasionally, sales were made by simply hanging out in the mall until a user spotted him. Then, through established non-verbal communication, Hoss and his customer would know when to get in the black Chevy truck and complete the transaction. In three days I knew all of his users, and I also knew Hoss' supply source.

My arrangement with Hoss was that I would pay for whatever junk I used, but I purchased it at only $10 a bag, which was $5 or $10 below market price. At this time, I was using about eight bags a day.

Besides being a dealer, Hoss was a heavy user himself.

Twenty minutes after he shot up, Hoss would invariably go "on the nod." Nap time was my opportunity to steal as much dope as I thought I could without him missing it. Like my dad, Hoss was a poor accountant. During the eight days I stayed with Hoss, I stole more "H" than I bought. I also stole a ton of money from him. He would just slump in his truck cab, and the money would be lying on the seat or sticking out of his shirt pocket, ripe for the picking.

In addition to outright stealing, I devised ingenious ways of obtaining money to support my habit. One of the things I did was sneak back into Dad's house through an unlocked cellar door after he left for a day at the office. I discovered a Lowe's receipt and copied the credit card numbers. Then I called restaurants all over town and ordered gift certificates. Some restaurants would redeem the certificate at face value. At others, I would be forced to order something from the menu in order to get change back in cash. My average daily take from using Dad's credit card numbers was approximately $100, still not enough to cover my current use costs. By this time, my usage had escalated to over ten bags per day.

Another favorite trick of mine was to call jewelry stores and pretend I was my dad, and order a gift certificate for my son, Adam. Often when I called, the clerk would inquire, "Is this Attorney Weaver?" to which I answered. "Yes." After that, the scam went through without further questioning and without a hint of suspicion.

On March 25, I called HM Rose Goldsmith and impersonated my father well enough to get a gift certificate for $350. I used the credit card numbers from the Lowe's receipt, and the transaction concluded without incident. Which was nice.

Next day, I walked out of HM Rose Goldsmith with $736.70 worth of jewelry thanks again to those wonderful credit card numbers. I tried the same scam on the third consecutive day, but the credit card didn't go through. Obviously, credit card security had wised up to me and put a block on the account. When the store manager asked me to wait, I took off. I knew he was headed for a back room to call the police. Anybody would have known that. I don't care who you are.

Later, I found out that representatives of USAA credit card, Fraud Detection Unit, had been tipped off by their computer because of unusual activity on the account. An investigator from San Antonio, Texas, telephoned my dad at his office to verify the legitimacy of so many recent purchases. An irregular use pattern was now appearing on the account, and the computer had been programmed to pick it up. Dad told the woman I must have surreptitiously obtained the account numbers and was not authorized to charge against the account. To prevent further thefts, the account was deactivated.

Dad refused to press charges against me because to do so would make more work for him and have no impact on me. It was lose-lose for him. He chose to pay the bill and forget it. Which was probably right.

As much as I feared courthouses, I went with Hoss to his Probation Violation hearing in Indiana County. The Probation Officer testified that Hoss was in technical violation of three conditions of his Order: (1) he failed his drug test; (2) he failed to report to his PO regarding a change of address; and (3) he failed to pay his fines and costs on the underlying drug offense.

The Presiding Judge, A. Ray Hugo, told Hoss he would listen to his side of the story before ruling. In reality, there was only one side to this story, and it had already been told by the PO.

Hoss wasn't worried that he had no explanation to give the Judge as to why he had not obeyed the Probation Order. He figured, worst case, to get 30 days, and he could do that time "standing on my head."

Worst case for Hoss became worse than expected. Judge Hugo revoked Hoss's probation and resentenced him to 11 1/2 to 23 months in the County Jail plus an additional $1,000 fine and loss of his street time. He ordered the Sheriff to take Hoss to the jail "forthwith."

I followed my friend to the holding cell where he talked the Deputy into allowing me to take possession of his Chevy truck. Then Hoss asked me if I would give his mother $1,000 he had hidden in the house. This would pay his fines and give him a chance to get out of jail early with credit for "good time." A good time modification of sentence is never considered unless all fines are paid. I reassured my friend, Hoss, that he could count on me to hand-deliver the $1,000 to his mother ASAP.

With Hoss safe in jail, I was swinging the world by the tail. I was driving his brand new black Chevy S10 pickup truck, living rent-free in his apartment, and I found almost half an ounce of cocaine and a brick of heroin. Adding good fortune to good luck, there was a roll of $20 bills, fifty of them, right where Hoss said they would be.

Two days later, Hoss called from jail saying he was going to "fucking kill" me for not delivering that $1,000 to his mother like I promised. A couple of months ago, when I was in the Westmoreland County Jail, my friend, Jordan, also said he was going to "fucking kill" me, and I thought at that time he might. Hoss' threat was hollow. By the time he got out of jail, all would be forgotten. Just the same, I tried to lie my way out of this one.

I told Hoss that I handed the money to his mother the same day he went to jail. Hoss replied that he just talked to his mom on the phone, and she never received the money. Indignantly, I told my friend that "his mother was a fucking liar!"

Hoss started going nuts on the phone. So I hung up. Who did that loser think he was talking to? Not even two weeks before, Hoss helped me steal $200 from my mom by telling her I needed money to pay my share of the rent. The way I figured, if Hoss can help me steal $200 from Mom, my stealing $1,000 from his mother is just getting even, and maybe a little better than that. Surely, Hoss must have known I would rip him off considering what we did to my mom. Probably he just did not like being a victim. For Hoss, the shoe was on the other foot, and he couldn't take it. Pussy!

Next day at the mall, I heard Hoss had hired muscle to work me over. Word spread that I got over on big Hoss for

$1,000 and ripped off all his dope. If suppliers were involved, matters could become ugly fast. I moved out of Hoss's place that afternoon.

My friend Nathan agreed to let me stay with him for a night or two, no more. Nate was pretty big into Oxycontin and didn't want anybody hanging out because some of his users were awful jittery around strange faces. Nate and Hoss were both hard core addicts. Neither was in the business for the money. Both sold to support their habits. The $1,000 I stole from Hoss went fast. Experience told me I would be all right without dope for a day or two before heavy withdrawal hit me. I asked Nate for a little bump, but he refused, telling me it was time, after only one night, for me to move on to another place.

I needed money, and I was running out of ideas. Asking Mom was out of the question. Security was wise to Dad's credit card numbers, which by now had been changed. After just ripping off Hoss, nobody on the street would trust me with an advance.

I went into the Boscov's store in the mall. My friend, Abby, worked the register in the housewares department. I talked to Abby for a few minutes, then made my move. I brought three clothing articles to her, a Polo T-shirt valued at $18.99, a Polo plaid dress shirt valued at $69.50, and Tommy Hilfiger jean shorts valued at $49.50. Abby removed the sensormatic tags from the clothes and rung up only the Polo T-shirt. She then placed all three articles of clothing in the bag and kept it at her register. Forty-five minutes later, I returned and picked up the bag. In the rear of the store I handed the goods to two black friends who paid me $25 to pull off the scam.

Unknown to any of us, the operation had been under surveillance by the Boscov's Loss Prevention Detective. As soon as the black men exited the store, they were stopped, and the police were summoned. The three of us were charged with the crimes of Conspiracy and Receiving Stolen Property. We were released at the scene and advised we would be receiving formal legal process in the mail. I thought "whatever", criminal charges are something I'll deal with later. Right then, I needed money for dope.

From Boscov's I went to Howard Brothers Hardware store. All sales attendants knew me from coming into the store with my dad to buy building materials, small hardware items, or tools. I selected an expensive circular saw and checked it out by simply signing a slip. The store would bill my dad later.

"Take care Adam." said Brian, one of the clerks.

"Say hello to your dad." said another as I left the store.

Immediately I walked across Hilltop Avenue to Hi-Way Electronics. The counter clerk informed me that because of the incident my dad had with Chuck, I was no longer permitted in the store. I handed the saw, which was still in the box, to my friend Tony and exited the store. A few minutes later, Tony came out of the store with $40 in his hand. With luck this would be enough to buy us each two hits. Which we needed.

While I was living with Hoss, I had access to plenty of heroin, most of which I stole when he was nodding. Since moving out, my use was curtailed, and I was down to one or two bags a day, which wasn't enough to prevent dope-sickness.

Next day I went back to Howard Brothers and bought an expensive drill. That was the third drill that was purchased there in just a few months; the hammer drill that I stole, the replacement, and now this one.

"You guys are wearing out a lot of drills over there, Adam." said Brian, only too willing to ring up the big sale and get my signature on the slip.

"Yeah, my dad loaned one and lost one." I quipped, placing the unopened box under my arm for the short walk to Hi-Way Electronics. There I would meet Tony to complete the transaction. We both pocketed $20, not bad for a drill that cost over $300.

My body weight dropped to 120 pounds. I was living on coffee and cigarettes, smoking almost three packs a day. There was an ever present bead of sweat across my upper lip. I felt itchiness everywhere and no place to scratch. My knees hurt and my back ached. Acne, which I had controlled with Minocycline, had now overrun my unshaven face. I had nothing: no friends; no job; no home; no money; no car; no future.

Unless Dad already sold it, the Ford Explorer would be in the garage. I needed wheels to help me get dope. With a car, I could reconnect with a supplier, like Stinky from Pittsburgh, and earn enough money to feed my habit. With luck, the cellar door to Dad's house just might be unlocked.

I checked every door on the house, and they were all

locked, even the basement door. Peering in the window, I could see Dad had completed a lot of work since I last helped him with the remodeling project. At twilight, the sun shining through the southwest basement window illuminated the cellar nicely. I turned to face the setting sun, and with my boot heel kicked the double pane glass out of the bottom sash. Then I reached in and unlocked the window and raised it so I could crawl through.

The bench Dad had built-in under the window provided an easy step down from the window opening. Once I got inside, I hurried upstairs to Dad's bedroom and hunted for money. Dad usually keeps a lot of money in the house for emergencies, so I figured my chances of scoring big were good. I rummaged through every dresser drawer but came up dry.

I bounded downstairs and checked the garage to see if my Ford Explorer was still there. It was! Keys to my Explorer were hanging on the top hook. Luck was with me.

Before driving away, I opened the armoire in the television room and reached behind the 17-inch Sharp model TV to unscrew the cable feed. Single handedly I loaded it into the Explorer. It took only a split second to unplug the Bose sound wave radio, and not much longer to carry that unit to the car. The engine fired on the first crank, and I backed my Ford out of Dad's garage. I was back in business.

My first stop was Tony's. From his place, we drove directly to Hi-Way Electronics to sell the TV and radio for a second time. The clerk must not have recognized these items, but he should have. After all, it had only been two or three weeks since these were the central objects of a dispute between Dad and Chuck, the store owner. Tony must have been a better negotiator than me, because he came out of the store with $300 for just the TV and the radio, whereas the best deal I could strike, which included the same TV, Dad's clock radio, Lisa's VCR, and an old stereo system was $275.

With my addiction now in full bloom, I went pro, living with a dealer in hotel rooms. He provided food and drugs, and I provided the transportation. It was a mutually beneficial arrangement. He figured the Drug Task Force agents would not recognize my Ford Explorer, and this gave him more freedom to move around.

It had been a while since I called my mom. Since I knew Dad would be looking for me, I stayed out of touch from her too, fearing she would disclose my whereabouts. I was certain Dad had already informed her about the break-in. I had a court appearance scheduled for April 11th in Pittsburgh and would have to come out of hiding then. I planned to call Mom a day or two in advance and ask for some travel money. She would resist and question me about kicking in Dad's window. I would have a hard time explaining why I stole the TV and wave radio a second time, but I'd tell Mom I needed wheels in order to get a job. That's what she wanted to hear me say.

Sure enough, the first person Dad called when he discovered the broken window was Mom. Not one to exaggerate, Dad believed I had reached the point with my addiction where I was capable of injuring or even killing another person in pursuit of drug money. For my own safety, and for the safety of others, Dad asked Mom to call the police and have me arrested as soon as contact was established.

On April 9, 2003, Mom called Dad at his office and told him I had left a message on her cell phone and would call her back at 4 that afternoon. Thinking fast, a plan to capture me was hatched and wheels put in motion. Dad told Mom to set up a 5:30 meeting at Denny's restaurant in Eastmont Township. The plan was to lure me into the blind parking lot with a promise of giving me cash for my Pittsburgh trip. Dad would block my escape route. At first Mom hesitated, protesting that in all her life she never lied to me. Dad told Mom that it would be a lie of necessity. "Would you rather lie to Adam, or find him dead?"

Instincts told me not to trust Mom when I talked to her and made arrangements to meet her for dinner. There was something shaky in her tone, not the usual comfortable conversation. Nevertheless, I needed money for the drive to Pittsburgh. Moreover, Mom would never lie to me. I agreed to meet her at Denny's restaurant at 5:30. At 4:20 Mom called Dad to confirm that the trap had been baited.

Immediately, Dad began implementing the capture plan. He asked Lisa if he could borrow her new white Audi four-door Sedan. Most likely, I would be looking for either a police unit or Dad's familiar green BMW. Lisa consented to the use of her car and also volunteered to ride as a passenger, in order to create the appearance of normalcy.

At 5:15 the white Audi slipped inconspicuously into the second row of parked automobiles in the old mall parking lot across the street from Denny's. From this vantage point, Dad and Lisa had an unobstructed view of the cut away to Denny's.

Even if I were on the alert and was trying to "dry clean" the area, it was not likely I would "make" their surveillance position.

Three times a dark green Ford Explorer cruised past Denny's, but did not enter the lot. On the fourth run, the left turn signal came on. Before the second blink had finished, Dad wheeled Lisa's Audi around the mall parking lot to execute the intercept.

I backed the Explorer into a parking space just in case this meeting with Mom was a set-up. Being street-smart, I wanted to be prepared for a fast getaway. It was too late. No sooner had I finished my maneuver than a white Audi pulled in front, boxing me in. My dad got out of the driver's side. His 5' 9" red-haired girlfriend exited from the passenger side. I stayed in my vehicle. Dad opened the driver's side door to the Ford. With his hand, he motioned for me to slide to the passenger's seat. I complied. My father spoke in serene tones.

"Please don't resist, Adam. We're driving up to the police station, and you're going to be taken to jail. I can't think of anything else that will give you a chance at life. If you decide you want to live, call me, otherwise, rot in jail. I hope you find the courage to make the right decision."

Sergeant Tom Dixon works full-time for Eastmont Township Police Department and part-time for Hilltop Borough. That explains how he was the same officer who responded to the incident between my dad and Chuck at Hi-Way Electronics, and how he was the duty officer at the Eastmont Police Station the night Dad brought me in.

I sat in the station on a steel folding chair in a concrete block room while Dad and Sergeant Dixon searched the Explorer. They found my works, two bags of dope and several articles of stolen clothing from various stores in the mall. I was photographed and fingerprinted and then told to wait for a cruiser to transport me to the Cambria County Prison. Fifteen minutes into the wait, I passed out due to physical and emotional exhaustion and fell to the station floor.

Sergeant Dixon recognized the extreme distress which caused the blackout. He asked my father, "Do you want me to call an ambulance, Dave?"

Dad replied, "No, Tom. He'll either make it or he won't."

Then Dad drove home.

Only Mortals Can Be Heroes

CHAPTER EIGHT

Hope Was On The Way

With the decline of coal and the disappearance of steel as backbone industries, Cambria County had fallen on tough economic times. One of the few newer buildings in the area was the prison. I guess I should have been thankful for a modern jail, but I wasn't. It made no difference whether the toilet was old or new. For the next six or eight days, I would become a frequent visitor to the head, either to vomit the contents of an already empty stomach or to respond to the cramps of an unceasing diarrhea. The drug demons were exacting homage as I knelt before their bathroom throne seized with involuntary, pulsating abdominal contractions which worked their way up or down the gastrointestinal tract, ending at a time and place of their choosing. Withdrawal does that to you.

In many respects, living behind bars in Cambria County was the same as being locked up in Westmoreland County. I was deprived of my freedom and forced to live on "the Man's" schedule. However, here in Cambria, I knew quite a number of inmates – druggies all of them. Fortunately, my buddy, Hoss, was doing time in neighboring Indiana County. So I didn't have to contend with that asshole. We bunked five to a cell, and there were no doors to the cells. Toilets were down the hall and were used on a first-come, first-serve basis. My friend, Jordan, from Westmoreland County, might not have approved this design, but to a person suffering withdrawal, a battery of community commodes was a majestic sight.

From the start, I was welcomed by my new cell mates, especially Larry. He was a black man approaching 40 and had a wide smile and funny way of talking. Larry's lighthearted, black dialect offered an amusing contrast to my father's lawyer language. I also respected Larry because he cared about me. When you're all alone in jail, about as low as you can get, it makes you feel good if someone cares about you. Everyone needs to believe someone cares about them. I don't care who you are.

After the bulk of the withdrawal symptoms passed, I started thinking about myself again, not just surface thinking, deep thinking. Was there a different and better life for me? Just because all of my friends ended up in jail or dead, must I be one of them? If I am God's special child, can I give myself a chance to find out what His plan is for me?

As I began thinking about a better lifestyle, I recalled my mom reading the story of "The Little Engine that Could." Against all odds that undersized locomotive was called upon to haul toys to children at camp on the other side of a big mountain. At first, the job seemed impossible. The grade was just too steep and the load too heavy. It looked like the children would not get their toys. When all seemed lost, the Little Engine began to believe that if it summoned all its strength and courage, perhaps it could pull the train over the top. As the Little Engine chugged up the mountain slope, it began to chant, "I think I can! I think I can!"

As a child, I jumped and squealed with glee when that Little Engine finally, after so much struggle, starting streaming down the other side of the mountain toward camp with a trainload of toys for the happy children. Why couldn't I be like "The Little Engine that Could" and climb that mountain? Fifteen years after Mom first read that story to me, the lesson sunk in. I started to say to myself, "I think I can! I think I can!" For the first time since I started drugging, hope was on the way!

Dad told me to call him when I was ready for help, but not until then. I could hear my father telling me no person ever won the Super Bowl by himself. Exactly how that applied to an addict wasn't clear, but the idea of getting others to help was starting to make sense to me. Retreating into my shell brought failure every time. Maybe there was a better solution than going it alone.

For two more days, I thought hard about calling Dad and asking for help. Part of me was afraid Dad would say "no," and part of me was even more afraid he would say "yes."

I discussed my fears with Larry. His opinion was straightforward.

"Adam, you call yo daa."

It took all my courage, and some of Larry's, for me to pick up the phone. I asked Dad if he would help me find a treatment center for my drug problem. I said I hated my life and wanted to explore drug treatment options.

Dad asked if I wanted to live. I replied that until very recently, I wanted to die. But now, I was willing to give life a chance. There was a pause. I think my dad was choking up but didn't want me to know, and since he was on the telephone, I couldn't see him. A few seconds later, Dad, speaking in a steady voice, told me how proud he was of me and how much courage it must take to face the challenge of defeating a drug addiction. I told Dad I didn't know anything about drug treatment. Dad told me not to worry because friends could direct us. He would start looking at treatment options tomorrow.

Before we hung up the phone, Dad told me he paid another visit to Hi-Way Electronics and reclaimed his 17" Sharp TV and Bose sound wave radio. He said he wanted to thank me for not taking the stuff too far away from home and hoped I had no plans to steal them a third time.

The first call Dad made was to his friend, forensic psychologist, Dr. Ray Dalton, to solicit his professional opinion concerning drug treatment. If anyone could provide helpful insight, it would be Dr. Dalton. At age 62, Ray had an impressive resume of successful practice in a number of areas including drug addiction and treatment. More significantly, Dr. Ray counseled me during my turbulent adolescence.

Dr. Dalton explained that the key to stopping my addiction is knowing what caused the behavior in the first place. Most addicts who go through treatment never discover the reasons they got hooked. There is no fail-safe test or method of diagnosing the source of addiction, but there are clues which could lead to a reliable diagnosis of causation, and therefore, better treatment planning.

Dr. Dalton was aware that when I was 13, I went through a period of rebellion and anger. I was beginning to get my man-strength and didn't know how to direct it. Slamming doors wasn't a sufficient outlet for my pent-up hostility and frustration. I preferred punching doors, and soon my hollow core birch bedroom door was destroyed by depressions and imprints from my fists.

One time, Dad's former girlfriend was present when I went into one of my punching tantrums on the door. When Dad tried to settle me, I told him I wanted a gun with two bullets, one for him and one for me.

Fortunately for me, Dad's girlfriend was a Mental Health professional with a Master's Degree in Counseling. She called Crisis Intervention, and within thirty minutes I was admitted for a two-week period of treatment at the Juvenile Psychology Ward at Central Hospital. I was diagnosed as severely depressed with suicidal and homicidal ideations. My condition upon release was "improved." After this I was put on Prozac, which never had any effect on me. Two years later, I quit taking it.

Feelings of inferiority coupled with a lack of self-worth characterized my adolescent years. Dr. Dalton recommended a barrage of positive feedback and reinforcement to help me get over this problem. In retrospect, throughout my life I got a lot of praise and encouragement from my family. So did Ben. I think maybe they went overboard in that direction.

Dad asked Dr. Dalton whether formal drug treatment was

necessary, or whether I could just make up my mind to quit drugging. Dr. Dalton pointed out that addiction to drugs, particularly heroin, is so overwhelming that I would have no chance of getting the monkey off my back unless someone was caring for me 24 hours a day. An addict cannot get clean unless he is given the opportunity to talk about his pain, not to just anyone, but to those who have experienced similar pain and are able to empathize with him. In-house therapy would be a big benefit for this reason alone. Peer support was essential. The longer I was kept clean, the closer I would come to being drug-free. Dr. Dalton explained that the DSM-IV definition for being drug-free is one year of full sustained remission from any drug.

Dr. Dalton had a theory that a link existed between addiction and adoption. It was probable, he thought, that my birth mother used drugs during her pregnancy, or before. However, I never met my birth mother and would have no way of knowing her drug use habits. Therefore, Dr. Dalton's addiction/adoption theory could not be proved in my case. Nevertheless, he speculated strongly that I was born with a "primitive memory of comfort." If the forensic psychologist's theory is correct, I became predisposed to use drugs even before I was born! Which is hard for me to believe.

Next day, I became part of a team that was assembled to choose a drug treatment center. Several fronts were opened. One of Dad's associates, Attorney Dan Walter, searched the internet for a listing of drug treatment facilities. Within two hours, Dan not only printed a listing of several hundred facilities, but had culled the list and highlighted the more promising centers.

The team gathered as much information as they could about drug treatment in order to match my needs with the program that offered the most hopeful opportunity for success. Although no dude ranches or ultra posh places were considered, price was a secondary issue in choosing the right center. Dad told me paying for drug rehab would be cheaper than letting me live at home, because no institution could exact a fee that cost more than what I could steal.

From the initial investigation, the team reached some quick conclusions. First, all were sobered by the abysmally low success rate of conventional drug treatment, which hovered in the five to fifteen percent range. Secondly, some studies suggested that no treatment at all was better than conventional treatment.

Talk about a formidable challenge! Our mission was to defeat a monster that was both evasive and difficult to kill. Compounding the problem, the only weapons in the armory had thus far proved ineffective.

We decided to conduct a broad search and compile a listing of drug treatment facilities. Since there was no reliable science to guide us, follow-up phone calls to these facilities would lead us to the right place, if not by science, perhaps by intuition.

Preliminary on-line searching pared the list of possibles to 20 institutions, including Mercy Behavioral Health, Peniel, Pyramids, Heartland, Greenbrier, and St. Jude's. Dad called all twenty on the list and asked questions directed at what he thought were the two most important issues: (1) the correlation between the length of treatment time with the success of outcome; and (2) the relapse rate at each institution.

Brochures were obtained from the more promising treatment centers. Others were eliminated after the initial contact. The reason Dad asked for brochures was that he wanted me to be the person who made the final decision, since I was the person who would be undergoing treatment. He mailed these pamphlets to me in prison where I could review the propaganda and decide which ones I preferred. It might have been easier if Dad had come to the jail and visited me, but as a matter of principle, Dad would not come to the jail. Mom was my only visitor.

One of the possibles was a popular facility that required an 18-month stay and was very churchey and regimented. Representatives wouldn't give success rates until my dad pressed, "Look lady, how can I ask my son to commit 18 months of his life to a program without knowing what his chances of success are?"

The woman reluctantly conceded, "The percentage is not very high. Not many are changed after the program. We don't keep statistics, but it's very low. Just a few do well."

After how I hurt my family, I would not have blamed them for giving up on me, but they did just the opposite. They lifted me up.

Uncle Ray and Aunt Lois checked the Pittsburgh Diocese to see if there were any religious-based treatment centers in the area. Uncle Walt and Aunt Nancy served as consultants.

Dad told me everyone in his office was on my team, including his legal assistants, Cindy and Jean, Attorney Dave Raho, and Attorney Dan Walter. This boosted my spirits. Mom and her family, Uncle Joe and Aunt Jan, Jeff and Steve were all praying that I could beat my addiction.

Considering I stole from Mom's family, as well as Dad's, I realized how lucky I was to have everybody's support. Was my family's willingness to put up with me a sign that they saw good in me, even if I didn't?

Most of my adult life was spent on the dark side, lying, stealing, cheating, and doping. My demeanor showed it. I walked around with slumped shoulders, hid my face under a hat brim, and always wore drab, oversized clothes. The mere thought of trying to succeed at anything scared me. I was consumed with self-doubt and self-pity. The time had arrived to take a stand. The choices were simple; either I try to make myself a better person and risk failure, or I just give up.

I got a letter in jail from Uncle Walt.

April 25, 2003

Dear Adam,

Your dad tells me that you are reflecting on your past failures and expressing some lack of hopefulness about future success. The question is: Is it good or bad to think about the past?

The answer is: YES it is. . .

It is either Good or BAD to think about the past. It all depends upon what you do with the "thoughts." If the thoughts result in increased self-realization they can be good. Because they will lead to understanding and renewed determination. If the thoughts lead to self- pity they will definitely be bad. Because they will lead to despair-which will accomplish nothing. It is a deadend.

Your dad says one of my ideas I gave him was important. I will try to tell it to you now. We are "determined" insofar as we "get" certain things given to us: born in poverty, a weak body which is prone to sickness, physical deformity, etc. But the second half of the equation is: What do we choose to do with the "stuff" we are given. This is the key. This is the part we "have to work with."

No person is immune to the influence of what he inherits, so to speak. But each person IS IN CONTROL of what he does with that "inheritance."

So let's assume that your birth mother was on drugs (a possibility, but not a certainty.) If this is a fact it can result in self-knowledge [or self-pity]. If it results in self-knowledge you can use that to understand the past (and understand some of the attraction of drugs) and at the same time use it to move forward. But you will not move forward using

> *transfer of blame or*
> *self-pity or*
> *victimhood or*
> *(heaven forbid) despair.*

You will move forward with:
> *understanding*

courage

the will to make something worthwhile of your time on earth.

Understanding that you are not the only person to "fail" can allow these positive things to take root and grow.

Here is a philosophical point. In the ancient myths there are Gods - who are immortal, and heroes - who must face life AND DEATH. Who are the more interesting? Not the Gods. Because they have nothing to lose, they have nothing to gain. Only the mortals can be heroes because only they must make choices which make life worth living, in difficult circumstances, with danger to themselves, in circumstances of uncertain outcomes, often in the face of danger and death.

On another point, a Jewish rabbi once wrote: God could have made it much easier for all of us to go through life, but perhaps he takes greater pleasure in seeing us struggle to overcome all the challenges of life – some of which are us ourselves! In the end greater joy comes not from dunking on the 4th grade team of the crippled children's home of the Little Sisters' school for the blind [no challenge] but from competing and even losing to a good or better team.

I had hoped to get you Elie Wiesel's <u>NIGHT</u>, which is an account of his time in a concentration camp as a young teenager. But the book store was out of it. I got <u>To Kill a Mockingbird</u>, because it is about INTEGRITY and courage (of the DAD) and I think also the daughters do not exactly understand why they have to read to the old lady who is not very nice to them. It is only later that they come to see that they were doing a great act of charity because she was on *dope to kill the pain of her cancer. The point being, we do not always understand things until later.*

St. Paul said, "we see now only in dark cloudiness, then we will see face to face." or "O God, how unsearchable are your ways and incomprehensible are your judgements." Trust me I have told God many times that He had better have a good answer for me about such-and-such when I face Him!

Nancy and I pray for you and your dad every day at meals.

> *Love,*
> *Uncle Walt*

After a thorough ten-day search, two treatment centers made the cut, Peniel, a local establishment, and St. Jude's Retreat House, situated in upstate New York, 450 miles away. Although Dad never told me outright that he favored St. Jude's over Peniel, I knew he did. So did I, mostly because I believed I needed to leave the area.

Before giving Dad the go-ahead signal to enroll me at St. Jude's, I talked the decision over with Larry. By now, I had come to respect Larry's wisdom. After hearing the pros and cons of Peniel versus St. Jude's, Larry said, "Did you ax yo Daa?"

"Dad likes St. Jude's."

"Then go wiff St. Jew. Sound better what others is."

Deciding on a treatment facility was the easy part. Next, I needed to hurdle a few legal obstacles. All plans hinged upon a jail release. One barrier included leaving Pennsylvania's jurisdiction to attend a "voluntary facility" in

New York State. Additionally, the court must view my situation at St. Jude's as "sufficiently custodial" to warrant my release. And finally, my release from prison had to be coordinated with the availability of a bed in the St. Jude's Retreat House.

Dad and Mom agreed to split the $6,950 tuition cost for the six-week residential program at St. Jude's Retreat House. If I chose to follow up on any of the Continuing Education programs offered by St. Jude's, the cost would be on Dad.

Amy, a young woman with a disarming personality, was the contact person at St. Jude's. When Dad first spoke with her, there were no rooms available until July. A few days later, Amy called back, reporting that there had been a cancellation, and that if I wanted the room, she could reserve it. Dad sent a $1,000 deposit and booked the room for May 23, 2003.

I didn't know about legal papers or motions filed with the court, but I got a Court Order releasing me from the Cambria County Prison on May 20. Dad told me the Judge wanted to send me directly to St. Jude's from jail, but he agreed to let me on the street a few days in order to give me enough time to have my teeth fixed.

Our family dentist squeezed me in on an emergency basis. He did ten or eleven restorations during my two mornings in the chair. I know I said, "Thank you." to Dr. Pappert as I left the office the second day, but as numb as my tongue was, it's questionable whether he understood me.

I packed that same carry-on bag for the trip to St. Jude's as I did when Dad kicked me out. I loaded up with a six-month supply of Tegretol and Minocycline and a couple bottles of vitamins.

While I was in jail, Uncle Dan helped Dad put three coats of polyurethane on the knotty pine boards in our family room project. The walls looked great. For lighting, there were eight wall sconces with alabaster shades to complement the drop light over the pool table. $3,500 worth of beautiful dark green carpet covered the floor. An old-fashioned, three-way floor lamp near the two new swivel chairs finished the job. I was proud of my contribution to the remodeling project. Which anybody would have been. I don't care who you are.

We spent the last evening at home, just Dad and I, shooting pool in our newly refinished basement.

We were playing Nine Ball, best of seven. Each of us had won three games, and it was the last rack of what we had dubbed the "Championship Game." I missed an easy combination shot on the nine which would have won the game and the match for me. It left the table set up for an easy run out for Dad to win the match. My father will never know, but I missed that shot on purpose, like he used to do when I was a kid.

Flipping Hotcakes

On May 22, 2003, we crossed the Pennsylvania-New York state line just south of Binghamton, me, Dad, and Uncle Dan. Six weeks of drug treatment in upstate New York would be my first extended time away from home. That assumes you don't count my excursion to the Florida panhandle in the spring of 2001.

Two years out of high school, and I was still shiftless and uninspired. Ben was in college and serving as a Military Policeman in the National Guard. All of my classmates were preparing to elevate their lives to another stage of responsibility and participation. Well, not all of my classmates, a few were druggies like me – going nowhere fast. Some were already dead.

Back in early '01, my friend, Nick, was similarly going nowhere. In some respects, he might have been in a little worse shape than me. Nick was living in a rickety mobile home in rural Somerset County, about six miles north of where Flight 93 crashed on 9-11. He was foolish enough to let some girl and her two-year-old kid shack up with him. Since neither

Nick nor I had anything positive happening for us at home, we cooked up a plan to drive to Panama City, Florida, and meet up with Nick's uncle. According to the uncle, jobs were easy to get in Florida.

I ran the Florida idea past my dad, and he liked it. "Do something, Adam. Take a first step. Even if you stumble, you'll learn." Mom was also in favor of me leaving to find work.

We loaded Nick's car, a sorry-looking Chevy Cavalier with an expired inspection sticker, worn down tires, and 173,000 miles showing on the odometer. Nick threw in the few bucks he saved from working as a Cable TV mechanic. Dad kicked in a $1,500 grub stake and Mom another $250. Then, down I-95 we headed, two dopers hell bent on having fun and hoping no job would get in our way.

As soon as we arrived at Nick's uncle's place, I called Dad to give him a contact telephone number. We planned to begin our job search the next day. Right! With money in our pockets, we didn't give two shits about finding work.

There were tons of hot girls gone wild in Panama City and tons of drugs to go with them. During that first week, Nick and I had plenty of both, but no jobs. Eight days into our search, we had already blown all of our money. Neither of us was interested in following up on any of the job leads the uncle had lined up for us.

Nobody knows what might have become of me had I not been transported to Bay Medical Center because of another separated shoulder. The shoulder went out during a seizure which came on because I failed to take Tegretol as directed. (When would I learn!) At the hospital, my shoulder was put back in proper alignment. They kept me under watch for one more day, then put my arm in a sling and released me.

While I was in the hospital, Dad informed me Pap had died. Nick and I drove north so I could attend the funeral. We were broke and doped, just like when we left home ten days earlier.

Thus ended my first excursion from home. Perhaps a couple months at a drug rehabilitation center in upstate New York would end on a happier note.

Although I didn't tell anybody, a large part of my decision to enroll at St. Jude's was to delay my sentencing on the pending Cambria County criminal charges. I also figured that completing drug rehab would influence the sentencing judge to lean my way a little bit. True enough, I hated jail and hated my life. But, I can't honestly say that my desire to get off drugs, which was more or less sincere at the time, was the primary reason I went to St. Jude's. Moreover, deep down I didn't think any of those clean-up programs worked. Why should St. Jude's? Several of my friends had tried getting clean, mostly at 28-day detox facilities where insurance pays. As far as I could tell, treatment didn't help any of them.

The first leg of our drive to St. Jude's ended at the Comfort Inn in Oneonta, NY. After breakfast at a '50's diner, Dad, Uncle Dan, and I drove the remaining 75 miles and arrived at our destination before 11 a.m. Finding the house was easy. It stood out, a gaudy Victorian structure with an American flag flying from a pole in the small front yard. To the south side a large deck was occupied by six or seven persons smoking cigarettes and drinking coffee. Behind the home was a gravel parking area. Beyond that we could see a volleyball court, which appeared to be worn into the ground pretty good, like our volleyball court at the cottage in Camp Sunshine.

As Uncle Dan led us through the vestibule, across an intricate patten of hardwood flooring into the parlor, a hand was extended, "Hi. I'm Steve from Roanoke."

Then another, "I'm Paul. I live in Rhode Island."

A third guy said simply, "Joshua."

"You're Adam. Nice to meet you. I'm Greg. I'm from Baton Rouge."

The sincerity and warmth of these unrehearsed greetings could not have been more welcome, especially for a guy like me, scared to death and having no idea what to expect. I had begun the journey, a boat without a compass in a storm-tossed sea. Greg, Paul, Joshua, and Steve tied tow ropes to my boat and tugged me into a safe harbor.

Just that quick I felt settled. No sense for Dad and Uncle Dan to hang around. A hug and a handshake was Uncle Dan's way of wishing me good luck. Then my dad gave me a hug of his own. As we embraced, he whispered in my ear, soft so nobody could hear. Dad said to remember I was God's special boy. He told me to dream and to pray, then he said he loved me. Dad kissed me, then he and Uncle Dan left to go home.

Daily life at St. Jude's was far different from what I expected. There were no hall monitors, no sign-out slips, no shift supervisors. There were only choices to be made and consequences which follow. I was not a patient in a ward. I was a guest in a home, just like 23 others.

Each day began with the choice of whether we wanted to board the van to the gym for an early morning workout or stay in bed to catch a few more winks. At St. Jude's I hit the gym almost every day, pumping iron with eight or ten other guys from the house. Our intense workouts lasted approximately one hour. My body grew strong, like it did when I had built myself up in jail to protect against an assault from sexual predators or nutcases like Jordan. Once again I started showing some impressive "guns." My self-image skyrocketed. Which it should have.

At home we had a complete gym set in our rec room with free weights, barbells, and cable machines. My dad encouraged me to develop my body as a way of increasing self-esteem. "Your body is a tabernacle, Adam. Treat it with respect." I wanted to work-out when I was home, but could never stay off drugs long enough to enjoy the benefits of habitual, consistent training.

After breakfast, I attended a morning class with one of the St. Jude instructors, and, in my case, one other guest. The guest was Michael, a 21-year old college student from Connecticut. Michael arrived one day before me, and we were paired throughout the six-week segment of the program.

Our instructor was a 42-year old black man from Newark, New Jersey. Calvin would be our "one on one" mentor for the balance of our stay at St. Jude's. Calvin, a former addict, carried 195 pounds of chiseled muscle on a five-foot-nine-inch frame. Physical bearing aside, what Michael and I really respected about Calvin was his ability to listen to our misdeeds and never show surprise, awe, or judgment. Calvin's response to even the most shocking revelations was soft-spoken and insightful. He himself was a veteran of the drug wars and had walked miles and miles in our moccasins. The three of us met daily for one 90-minute class in the morning and another in the afternoon. Evenings were free except for the 45-minute seminar at 8 p.m. which was mandatory for all the guests.

The first lesson Calvin taught Michael and me was that we were not at St. Jude's to be treated or rehabilitated from an incurable disease. Such an approach would condemn us to living one miserable day at a time. We were there to be educated, to learn how to live happy, fulfilled lives governed by choices we could control. This approach placed the outcome in our hands and offered hope, but no guarantees.

During our classes, I spoke freely in front of Calvin or Michael. They appeared to be just as open with me. There was nothing to be gained from being secretive or closed, and everything to lose. A tight bond based on shared experiences soon formed among the three of us. Sometimes during our discussions, Calvin revealed an uncanny insight about me, as though our brains were hardwired. We communicated emotions, sensations, and intuitions at a level that could be attained only by another person who had "been there and done that." The connection among the three of us was so intimate as to create a unique species of clairvoyance, which at times produced an uneasy feeling.

Calvin doubled as my personal trainer at the morning weightlifting workouts, always ready to give me a little spot if it looked like I couldn't make the lift. Soon he began calling Michael and me his "sons." He watched over us and protected us as any father would. We affectionately referred to Calvin as "Pops."

Shortly before I left for St. Jude's, Dad got another phone call from Ben, who was still in Saudi Arabia. Ben said he expected his National Guard unit to be returning to the states within thirty days. Therefore, all soldiers were instructed to send bulky items ahead by separate carrier because they could not be shipped on the troop transports.

Ben forwarded two parcels. In one box, he shipped his souvenirs and presents. The other had the unmistakable appearance of a woman's figure, but was more likely a guitar box. Dad put both boxes in Ben's bedroom, leaving them sealed in order for Ben to enjoy the ceremonial opening when he came home. What Dad didn't know was that I had two free days between my jail release and my trip to St. Jude's. This provided ample time to sneak into Ben's room and cut around the edge of the guitar box, flap it back, and remove the guitar. I carefully resealed the box as if it had not been disturbed. This was Ben's second acoustical guitar, the one Dad mailed to him after I stole the first one. This guitar found a home at Music Haven. Scratch guitar number two.

Lucky for me I was 500 miles away when Dad and Ben discovered I stole the second guitar. Actually it was the third, if you count the green electric Stratocaster that Dad didn't know I took. I remember how ballistic my father went upon discovering that I took the first one, and I'm still not sure why he didn't flatten my head against the door jamb for that.

Neither Dad nor Ben ever mentioned the stolen guitars. What good would it do? Knowing Dad, he bought Ben a third guitar, better than either of the two I stole. Probably Dad told Ben there is no sense in him suffering just because I have a problem. In a way, my loving brother should thank me for stealing his guitars. Each time I sold one for crack, he got an upgrade.

Life at St. Jude's was fun. In addition to the weekday fellowship of the guests, we enjoyed weekend outward-bound experiences. Of these activities, my favorite was the mountain hikes. The Adirondacks were right in our backyard, and we had a hundred or more trails from which to choose. After a day on the mountain, food tasted better, and sleep came easy. A "high" of its own.

We also enjoyed water sports, particularly rafting. There were some nice class-three rapids on the Hudson River about sixty miles north of Albany. The whole gang of us would pack into the van and drive to our riverside destination for an afternoon of paddling and splashing, and later, a picnic.

Rafting the Hudson brought back memories of Uncle Dan's annual rafting trips on the Youghiogheny River back home in Pennsylvania. Every June, when the river was swollen from spring rains, Uncle Dan's "Adventurer's Club" shot the Yough in 6-man rafts. Compared to the Yough, the Hudson was calm, but it was just as much fun rafting with my friends from St. Jude's as an adult as it was rafting the faster water with Uncle Dan as a youngster.

Weeks three and four of the program were devoted to writing our life stories. The idea was to air out dirty laundry, to pick scabs off old wounds so they could heal from the inside-out.

My story began with my adoption. When you're adopted, you're going to question why you were given up. Anybody would wonder about that. I don't care who you are.

As my mind pondered the complexities of my adoption, time and again a theme of worthlessness emerged. If I had value, why was I given away? How could I feel loved, if I was rejected by my own mother before I ever had a chance to prove to her that I was worth keeping. On the other hand, maybe my birth mother was right to give me away. I had done nothing in life to make her regret giving me up.

Under Calvin's guidance, I learned a different way to think about all the issues caused by the fact that I was not the flesh and blood of the persons I now called mom and dad. Calvin told me to flip the hotcake and look at what might be on the other side. In the black community, people are loved because of who they are, not because of birth status. If birth status were the measuring stick, too many blacks would be unloved. My own birth status could have included other possibilities, besides rejection, that influenced my birth mother to offer me for adoption. It could be that my birth mother was too young to properly raise a child. It could be that my birth mother was poor and wanted me to have a better life than she could provide. Slowly I was trying to understand that being adopted doesn't necessarily mean I was rejected. It might mean the exact opposite. If I considered these other possibilities, maybe I would come full circle and understand my adoption as a gift from my birth mother to me, perhaps the ultimate gift, the gift of life.

I wanted to be happy, and I was trying. Still, it is hard to be happy if you can't accept the circumstances surrounding your birth. Talking with Calvin and actually writing my thoughts on the pages of my workbook illuminated his point, that there was more than one way to view the adoption issue. He was right about the hotcakes too. Sometimes Grandma would let her hotcakes get too dark and one side, but when she flipped them over to the golden brown side, they looked and tasted a whole lot better.

Calvin taught Michael and me a concept called "The Four Absolutes": Love, Honesty, Purity, and Unselfishness. Using honesty as a basis for writing my life story would not allow me to make excuses for my choices. My brother, Ben, was adopted just like me, and he was no doper; doofus yes, doper, no!

The fact that Ben and I were raised together took away any blame I might place on my parents. I could not honestly say my parents caused me to become an addict. I did that to myself. Adopted or not, I had to begin accepting responsibility and holding myself accountable for my behaviors. After all, nobody picks his parents. All of us are stuck with who we get. Life, in this respect, is a throw of the dice. Infants don't get to choose their mother and dad any more than they can choose the color of their hair, or their race, or gender, or whether they will be athletic, or any other trait. Uncle Walt was right. The challenge is to make the most of who you are with the cards you have been dealt.

An indispensable part of learning to be happy is making amends, and I had plenty of mending to do because of all the people I hurt over the past 12 years. Perhaps my most sinful offenses came against those who loved me the most. What a harsh irony it is that this should be true.

Sixty-three years ago, Grandma and Pappy Kuncelman got married in a small church in northern Cambria County. Grandma wore the rings Pappy gave her for all these years. On a summer afternoon in 2002, the time came when Grandma would wear the rings no more. After Sunday dinner, when the Kuncelman family retreated to the sunporch, I struck. The rings were sold for dope.

Grandpa Weaver loved ocean-going vessels, probably because they reminded him of sailing around the world during his World War II service. Nobody could hold your attention like Pap when he started spinning stories about his days at sea.

In 1998, Pap and Grandma spent a week aboard the Caribbean cruise ship, Inspiration. At the island stop of St. Thomas, Pap, not the romantic type, bought a $500 gold chain as a present for Grandma. She cherished that 14-carat gold memory of happy times with Pap.

The gold necklace became all the more precious to her after Pap passed away, ending a marriage that lasted 62 years. Within six months of his death, the chain was gone, sold as second-hand jewelry to an underhanded jeweler so I could take a few more puffs from a crack pipe. Once again proving that no one or no thing mattered to me except my next high. I was selfish and would do anything to get what I wanted.

My dad and Uncle Walt were visiting Grandma one Saturday morning when, crying and heartbroken, Grandma told them her gold chain was missing from its case and that I probably stole it. Immediately I was summoned to Grandma's house. There I became the subject of a relentless inquisition, but I held up under the ensuing brow-beating and did not admit to stealing the gold chain. Denials got me nowhere. I have never seen Uncle Walt so angry. My dad walked outside with me, then literally threw me off Grandma's porch into the yard. Then he booted me out of his house for the third "and final" time.

Neither of my Grandmas has enough years left for me to atone in deed for the deep hurt I brought them, nor could I ever adequately assuage their grief with words. To say, "I'm sorry," no matter how sincere, would be insufficient. Saying, "I love you, Grandma," would be better, but still not good enough.

There are just some things in life you can't take back. I resolved to make amends as best as I could and, from this point forward, to add a little joy to their lives, and hope that a joyful heart is a little quicker to forgive.

The month of June 2003 was coming to an end. Nobody at St. Jude's was prepared to pronounce me drug-free after only five weeks. A 12-year drug addiction does not remit over so short a period. Both Calvin and Michael recommended that I try to enroll in the three-month Continuing Education Plan, especially since I had only begun to understand the pleasures of life without drugs. I talked to my dad and asked if he would consider paying the additional cost to allow me to stay at St.

Jude's for three more months.

Without hesitation, Dad agreed to extend my stay, providing he could arrange a concurrent delay of the sentencing, which he thought he could. In the meantime, Dad was planning to visit me. He wanted to decide for himself whether or not I was benefitting from the program. I was eager for Dad's visit and couldn't wait to show him that he got his son back after a long leave of absence. I hoped he would be proud of me.

On the last day of June, a package with no return address was delivered to me by UPS. At first I thought it was a box of Aunt Lois' hand-dipped chocolate covered raisins (she knows raisins are my favorite), but the box was too light. If not Aunt Lois' candy, then what? And from whom?

Back in my room I opened the package and found a present from Dad with a note congratulating me for completing the intensive six-week program. The present was a Seiko watch with a masculine black dial set off by gold numerals. I loved it!

That week I also got a card from Mom, telling me how proud she was of me. Mom reassured me that she and her husband Tom would visit me soon.

CHAPTER TEN

"Yes, Your Honor"

On the first Saturday in July 2003, our morning bull session on the Retreat House deck was interrupted by the unmistakable "potato potato" sound of two 1,450 cc Harley-Davidson V-twin engines. Glancing up Church Street, we spied a pair of Heritage Softail Classics rumbling toward the house. Slash-cut Screamin' Eagle exhaust pipes rudely burped and gurgled progressively louder as the machines neared. The man on the red bike was traveling solo, but the driver of the teal colored cycle was riding two up. Quiet resumed when the black suited drivers hit the kill switch after backing their motorcycles off the street in front of the Retreat House.

First off the bikes was Uncle Dan, driving the flashy red one. Next, Dad set the kickstand on his chromed up machine and leaned it to the left. He steadied the bike so his red-haired passenger could swing her long leather leg across the Mustang seat for a safe dismount. Boots, goggles, helmets, riding gloves, and a red, white, and blue doo rag completed the getup. Lisa, a professional woman, enjoyed playing the role of biker bitch, and she was soooo good at it.

The motorcyclists rested at the house for a short 30 minutes. Then I strapped on a helmet and climbed on the back seat of Uncle Dan's Heritage Softail. We headed due east to Vermont with plans to spend the whole day touring. Two hours later, the cycles cruised into Bennington. There was a museum at the edge of town that Dad had visited 30 years ago featuring a number of Grandma Moses original paintings. Knowing Uncle Dan is an art aficionado, Dad put the art exhibit on our must-see list. I didn't think I would like walking through a gallery, but I did. Viewing priceless artwork was as good a way to stretch our legs as any.

Our stop-over coincided with "Bennington Days." The whole town was decorated with flags and banners, antiques were on display everywhere, and the townsfolk walked about in colonial attire. The ladies flaunted flowing dresses with puffed shoulders and colorful bonnets. Men wore either frontier animal skin suits or simple Amish-looking farmer outfits with broad-brim hats and white cotton shirts.

As our bikes quietly choked their way out of town on low throttle, we enjoyed the unexpected treat of coming upon a company of Revolutionary War re-enactors who were putting on a show commemorating the Battle of Bennington.

Our route home took us through five covered bridges and two thunderstorms. Since we were running late, we climbed into rain suits and powered head first into the storm cells, which were approaching from the west. This was my first experience wearing rain gear while riding a motorcycle, and I learned rain suits do a good job of creating the illusion of dryness. We arrived back at St. Jude's saddle sore and wet. It was a good feeling.

Before they left, I introduced Dad, Lisa, and Uncle Dan to Michael, Calvin, and some of the other guests. While Uncle Dan and Lisa chit-chatted with my friends, Dad and I finalized my plans to extend my stay at St. Jude's for three more months. Dad said the judge authorized me to remain in the program. Acting on orders from the judge, the Court Administrator postponed my sentencing until October 28, 2003. In the interim, the long arm of the law still had me under court control.

In some respects, I was relieved that the law had finally caught up with me and that my day of reckoning had been set. With all the stealing, cheating, and lying I had done, bringing me to justice was just a matter of time. Waiting for the hammer to fall only added to my stress.

The Commonwealth of Pennsylvania had charged me with having committed 44 separate crimes. These included: forgery, felony; theft by deception, misdemeanor; criminal conspiracy to receive stolen property, misdemeanor; receiving stolen property, misdemeanor; unauthorized use of automobile, felony; possession with intent to use drug paraphernalia, misdemeanor; criminal attempt to commit credit card fraud, felony; credit card fraud, felony; bad checks, misdemeanor.

This long list of charges did not include the Criminal Complaints which had been filed against me in three other Western Pennsylvania counties. Drug charges were pending in both Allegheny and Westmoreland Counties, and theft and forgery charges were brought in Blair County.

Even though I realized my sentencing could not be

postponed indefinitely, I was worried about that October 28th court date. Anybody would have been worried if they had to go before a judge with my list of offenses. I don't care who you are.

Most of the forgery charges were for bad checks I had written against my brother Ben's account. In August, 2002, when Ben left for Saudi Arabia, I went into his room and found his checkbook and his expired driver's license. That's all I needed to raid his account.

Ben made arrangements to have his military pay deposited directly into his bank account back home. That worked swell for me. Each month, the account was automatically replenished with money Ben earned pulling security duty at an airbase in Riyadh. From his position half-way around the world, there was no way for Ben to know I was accessing his account. As fast as the Army auto-deposited Ben's monthly salary, I auto-withdrew it. During a three or four-month spree, I wrote 30 or 40 checks against Ben's account totaling over four thousand dollars. A more perfect scheme could hardly have been arranged by design, and I just lucked into this one.

Problems surfaced after I got greedy and overdrew the account. This triggered a bank investigation. Notices were sent to Ben for his input, but he was in a combat zone, which hampered communications. Four months passed before sufficient information was exchanged to get the mess sorted out and to identify me as the perpetrator.

In addition to draining Ben's bank account, the overdraws caused damage to Ben's credit rating. Various credit collection agencies started sending nasty letters to Ben's home address, demanding payment for items HE allegedly purchased when, in fact, I had bought the stuff by posing as my brother using his expired I.D. In order to protect my brother's credit, Dad wrote letters to a number of agencies trying to explain the bizarre circumstances that gave rise to Ben's suspect credit status.

The overdraws and the unpaid bills also touched off a cluster of telephone calls. Mean-spirited collection agents ignored the law and called at inconvenient hours. Our home phone would ring two or three times a day with a collection agent on the other end. Phone fights evolved into a source of modest amusement. All I could hear was Dad's side of the conversation:

"Ma'am, would it be possible for you to leave your home telephone number? That way I could call you at a more convenient time, say, during your family dinner hour."

(Pause)

"No, Ma'am, I'm not trying to be a wise guy with you. You just caught me at a bad time."

(Pause)

"That's right, Ben is overseas in the military. He did not make the purchase."

(Pause).

"I'm not responsible for Ben's account. He doesn't live here, so please don't call here anymore."

(Pause)

"Ma'am, can you answer this question: 'Why do all credit

collectors have to pass the asshole test as a condition precedent to getting hired?"

(Shorter pause)

"Well, certainly, I'm calling you an asshole. That's what you are! A flaming asshole!"

(Click)

Two years after the fact, Dad still got an occasional collection call.

Another problem arose in mid-September, 2003. Near completion of my three-month continuing education program, I was feeling sluggish and run-down. Usually, I was the trail blazer who led the group to the summit when we went hiking, and I was the man who volunteered for the heavy lifting around the retreat house. But lately, my supply of energy had petered out. Little by little, week by week, I began to tire. By early October my body did not respond to rest. I called my dad and explained the symptoms.

"Adam, did you ever share a needle with a junkie?"

"Yeah, Jason Meyer."

"Then you have hepatitis." Obviously, "Doctor Dad" reached a quick diagnosis.

After a pause, my father allowed himself a brief moment of lost composure, "You and your goddamned drugs! What other problems would you like to cause, Adam? You have damaged relationships. You have ruined your health. Your reputation isn't worth a shit. Nobody trusts you. You cost me a fortune and took 20 years off my life. Now, you'll never pass an employment physical because of hepatitis. What the hell more can you possibly think of to destroy?"

There was another pause, a bit longer than the first one. I expected Dad to continue venting his frustrations like he usually did, but he came back subdued.

"Adam, I'll call Fred and ask if he will test your blood when you come home for sentencing next month. The blood test will confirm my suspicion that you have hepatitis – but you do."

Then it was Dad's turn to relapse, "Goddamn it, Adam! That's another $400 dollar bill shot in the ass just for blood tests. You and your goddamned dope!"

Because of my history with addiction, multiple hospitalizations for overdosing and for shoulder procedures, head tumor, and history of seizure activity, we could not find a health insurance carrier who would cover me. For a brief time in the summer of '01, I got green card coverage through the state. However, as soon as I reported an $8 an hour job at the Carpet Warehouse, the State yanked my medical coverage. Fortunately, we lived in a close-knit town and most of the doctors who treated me knew me or my dad. Some worked on me and never sent a bill. Others reduced their fee or worked out terms of payment with my dad, I guess.

After some calmer discussions, we decided to take immediate action on the assumption that I did in fact have Hep-C. Precautions were necessary to guard against the inadvertent spread of the virus from me to an innocent third party at the guest house. Ironically, here I was worried about one of my friends at the Guest House catching hepatitis from me, but eight months earlier I stuck a filthy needle into my veins immediately after Jason used it, knowing Jason was infected! I can't explain why I played Russian roulette with a dirty needle, except to say that at the time all I thought about was the warm feeling of a body flush with the smooth pleasure of dope. Viewed from the standpoint of a drug addict, my risky behavior was understandable. A heroin addict who is getting ready to shoot will NEVER refrain for fear of catching hepatitis.

Dad told me that he had a lawyer friend, Brent, in California who beat hepatitis with heavy doses of Vitamin C, a routine of healthy living, no smoking, sensible diet, regular exercise, and no alcohol. We figured if Dad's 55-year-old friend could beat hepatitis, so could his 22-year-old son. Calls were made the next day to California for details. Brent explained that he took 10,000 milligrams of Vitamin C daily. He also drank eight or more glasses of water each day and got plenty of sleep. The idea was to give the liver a chance to heal itself. After following this routine for ten years, Brent's body was completely free of the hepatitis virus. Brent's success was encouraging.

Taking the information Brent provided a step further, a second computer search was launched with the mission: Find out if there is a Magic Bullet that will help me recover from still another self-inflicted wound.

In the meantime, Dad said he would talk to our neighbor, Dr. Fred, and inquire whether modern medicine could help.

Fred explained that the conventional drug therapy for Hepatitis-C was a regimen of Alpha Interferon in combination with Ribavarin. A quick check of the Physician's Desk Reference showed side effects, one of which was skin rash and acne, a second was depression. Since I suffered from depression most of my life and was having acne problems, Interferon seemed like the perfect drug not to take. Dad and I agreed that conventional treatment could be practiced on somebody else, but I would explore other options.

Two weeks later, I got my first shipment of supplements from Alternative Medicines Solutions, INC. which included milk thistle, dandelion root tea, and a substance called Siliphos, which supposedly provided liver support and protection. The first batch cost Dad $389.35. I promised to take the supplements as directed and to quit smoking.

My fingers must have been crossed behind my back when I made those promises. The dandelion root tea tasted like horse piss, and I wouldn't drink that stuff even at the point of a spear. As for smoking, every one of the guests at St. Jude's smoked cigarettes. With others smoking in front of me all the time, was it humanly possible to quit?

By September 30, 2003, I had completed my Continuing Education phase, and I was in line to enter the St. Jude Retreat House Intern Program. There were no guarantees that I would become an instructor, but that was my hope. To be selected, I had to demonstrate my capabilities in competition with a number of others for limited positions.

While I was interning, Calvin's parents came to visit him. Calvin introduced Michael and me to his folks as his "sons." We enjoyed an afternoon visit with Pops and his mother and father. They were concerned about Calvin, just like my mom and dad were concerned about me, and they drove from New Jersey for reassurance. Nothing beats seeing, face to face.

Calvin himself had been waging a hard fought battle against drugs. Whether drugs or Calvin would emerge the victor was still uncertain.

My anxiety level heightened as the October 28th sentencing date neared. That was another psychological stressor I had to deal with because of my doping, a nagging consequence of twelve years of selfish living. I wondered how it would feel to have my mind free of stress. In my entire adult life, I went from fear to fear, lie to lie, never knowing mental peace.

Two days before my court appearance, Michael drove me home for my court date. We tried to enjoy the ride and really didn't talk too much about what might happen at the sentencing on Monday morning. The Sentencing Memorandum of Law had already been submitted, and there was nothing more anybody could do, except wish me good luck. We decided not to raise unnecessary anxieties over the unknown. There are enough real monsters for us to contend with in life. No need to create more.

October 28th arrived on schedule. Nervously, I put on an oxford cloth dress shirt and laced the tie through the button down collar. In an hour, I would be standing before President Judge D. Gerard Long in the Court of Common Pleas of Cambria County for sentencing. If the worst happened, I would take it like a man. One of the lessons I learned at St. Jude's was to be more accepting of things I could not control. Just the same, I prayed the Judge would have mercy on me and not send me back to jail.

My case was called, and I stood at a podium six feet away

from the bench, with my Dad to my left representing me. A sturdy Deputy Sheriff with big biceps stood behind me. Judge Long looked toward the District Attorney and said, "Let's hear some facts."

The District Attorney began reading from the Criminal Informations, telling the Court the specific criminal conduct I engaged in for each charge. "To the charge of 0377 of 2003, forgery, a felony of the second degree, the defendant did on or about October 8, 2002, with intent to defraud and injure one Wal-Mart, and with knowledge that he is facilitating a fraud or injury, make, complete, execute, authenticate, issue, or transfer any writing, to wit: he did cash check number 272, made payable to Wal-Mart in an amount of $42.08 drawn on the checking account of one Benjamin Weaver, so that it purports to be the act of said Benjamin Weaver, who did not authorize that act, all of which is against the Act of Assembly and the peace and dignity of the Commonwealth of Pennsylvania."

After the first case was read, my Dad interrupted, "Excuse me, Your Honor. It will not be necessary to read the entire list, case by case. We will stipulate to the accuracy of the information set forth in the charging documents."

Later, I asked my dad why he agreed to all the facts, and Dad said it was never good psychology to allow the prosecutor to repeat the specifics of the crime at a sentencing hearing. This could only serve to stir up passions that are better left dormant.

At this point, Judge Long looked at me and asked, "Do you admit that you committed these crimes?"

I answered, "Yes, Your Honor."

"Why don't you turn around and tell those school kids sitting over there why you decided to become a criminal?"

Talk about pressure! At that moment, I almost took another seizure. I was not prepared to address school kids. I was ready to explain my reasons for becoming a criminal to the Judge, not that I had any good reasons, but I intended to tell him that my conduct was being driven by an indescribable need to get money for drugs. Of course, that was not the kind of explanation the Judge was asking me to tell these kids. Making matters worse, there were at least 75 high school students present on the day of my sentencing. If I messed up, I could really get hammered.

My mind raced as I hurriedly rearranged my thoughts and began speaking.

"I'll try as best as I can to tell you how I got started on drugs. I can't say I'll get the story perfect. Mostly I wanted to fit in and be accepted. To me, it was cool watching an older guy do dope, sort of like a rebellion against people who laughed at me. When I used drugs, I could laugh back at them. At first, it was fun and made me feel happy to get high. After a while it wasn't fun. Yes, the dope was fun, but I was starting to feel alone, as if I was the only person alive. I didn't even want to be around my family, and I have a great family. So, I hope nobody here is using drugs, because if you are, you'll end up in jail, like I was; or dead, like five of my friends. So that's about it."

County Probation prepared a Presentence Investigation

Report containing background information such as my health, family status, level of education, prior criminal history, and financial circumstances. The Judge asked if I had read that report, and I nodded affirmatively. He was only moments away from slamming the gavel. Blood rushed to my head, but I stood solid, ready to take my punishment.

On the way to the Courthouse that morning, my dad told me he would like me to do just one thing when I was sentenced, and that was to maintain my composure. At this point, there was nothing I could do to change the sentence, so it was imperative that I not lose dignity by appearing unduly shaken. If the sentence came down heavy, then I had to draw on my character reserves at the front end in order to make it through to the back end. If the sentence came down light, it would be because the Judge saw something in my background that held out hope for me, and a jubilant display of emotion would be equally wrong. A poker face was called for.

As it worked out, I got sentenced to pay a fine, court costs, full restitution to those persons from whom I stole money, three months in jail with credit for time served, and five years probation.

I could not have hoped for a better outcome. The worst part of the sentence was paying the fines and court costs. All together, these items added up to almost seven thousand dollars. But that was only money. The good news was I didn't have to serve any additional jail time. And I was still alive.

As for paying the costs and fines, Dad liquidated a savings account he held in trust for me. This account had a balance of $6,000, leaving me $1,000 short. The court made arrangements to put me on a payment plan to cover this shortfall, but, since I had no income, my dad was the person who was put on the payment plan. Dad also reimbursed Ben the $4,000 I stole from his bank account when he was overseas.

I had done some calculations in my mind, trying to figure how much it had cost my dad so far because of my drugging. The figure was close to one hundred thousand dollars, not counting the money I stole from my mom and the others, or the money Mom spent trying to help me. On second thought, 100 grand wasn't nearly enough to cover my costs!

After he sentenced me, Judge Long told me he was pleased that I was trying to address my drug addiction. He placed right on the record that if I stayed out of trouble for the next two years, he would consider shortening or even terminating my probation. Indeed, Judge Long must have seen something in me that he liked. Which was good.

Arrangements were made through the Office of Adult Probation for me to return to upstate New York to complete my internship. By now, I had finished an intensive six week social/educational program as well as the three months Continuing Education curriculum. The Court found no good reason to interrupt my progress by confining me to the State of Pennsylvania. Technically, my probation should have been transferred to New York before I left Pennsylvania. But, sometimes even the court brushes aside red tape requirements that get in the way of progress.

CHAPTER ELEVEN

Homecoming

Winter comes early in the Adirondacks. Days don't last long and nights seem endless. Above the clouds, the sun still shined, but we seldom got to see sunshine after December rolled in. On top of this, I was getting homesick.

Except for a three-day leave for sentencing in late October, I had been in upstate New York continuously for over six months. Thoughts of returning to my Pennsylvania roots popped into mind soon after Judge Long sentenced me. Part of my reason for going away in the first place was to delay sentencing for as long as I could. Now that I knew I wasn't going back to jail, I began thinking of going home.

Michael was against it. So was Calvin. Neither thought I was ready to return, especially without a long-term plan, but stubbornness was one of my character flaws that I decided to keep. Subtle changes in my attitude emerged. I was reverting into my former persona. Instead of flipping the hot cakes to the golden brown side, I let the burned side up.

The St. Jude administration was rushing to complete remodeling of an old hotel in Wells to accommodate a growing number of applicants. These persons had to be placed on a waiting list because there were not enough beds in the mother house. At one point, one person on the waiting list died from a drug overdose. Most of us guests took this loss personally, and the tragic news created a sense of urgency to make more beds available.

All through November and December, I labored 12 hours per day on the Wells Hotel remodeling project. Whatever job was most pressing at the time was the job I performed. With sledge hammers and crow bars I knocked down partition walls. I stepped on nails, cut my fingers, and blistered my hands. I stained oak trim, stuffed insulation, framed bunk beds, rough-plumbed showers and lavatories, and hung hundreds of sheets of drywall. Difficult jobs and dirty. Aching muscles and a sore back were my way of answering the pleas of my brothers and sisters who were waiting.

I endured until December 21, 2003. The way I figured, there was a limit to the concept of service to others. Three months of back-breaking servile work without a paycheck had broken me. Besides, my status as instructor was still in question and, instead of reassurances from top brass, I got vague answers to my inquiries about when I would be granted full-time status as a paid staff member, as most interns did not get paid until after a full year of volunteering.

A year ago at Christmas time, I was in a cold cell in the Westmoreland County Jail with my friend, Jordan. This year I would spend Christmas at home with my family. Yes, I was in charge of myself now! It was time to go home.

Two weeks before I decided to go home, I began to hear

the sound of distant drums, calling me from far away in the back of my mind. In times of stress, the drumbeat grew louder, causing me to become more unsettled. My resolve to stay clean was being challenged by those same self-created thoughts which in the past had so easily seduced me. For seven months at St. Jude's, I resisted these secret stirrings, bolstered by fellowship and support of guests and staff as close as the person in the bottom bunk. Calvin and Michael were book-end protectors who watched over me, sideline to sideline. Under their care and with their support, I would not fail; I could not let them down.

On the afternoon of my departure from St. Jude's, Calvin walked me to the car. He grabbed me with his thick black arms and hugged me tight as if to say, "Don't forget Adam, I'm your Pops, and I'll always be here for you." I hugged him back with all my might to let him know he had done all he could for me, and it was time for me to fly away.

We stepped back, and this time Calvin spoke out loud, his baritone faltering a little, "Thank you, Adam, for becoming part of my life. You'll never know how good you made me feel. You are a special son to me."

Calvin was talking to me with the same voice as if my own dad were talking. At that moment, I understood I had learned to love another human being. I could think outside the sphere of selfishness that surrounded my former life. As I got in my car, homeward bound at last, all sorts of emotions played across my psyche. What in the world had happened to me at St. Jude's!

When I got home, the Christmas tree was standing but not

decorated, nor were the outside displays in place. Those jobs fell to me, and I was glad to lend a hand. As hoped, Christmas 2003 was very special.

As soon as the holidays passed, Dad and I talked seriously about the decisions I had to make with regard to my future. He viewed my present circumstances with optimism. Which I might have expected.

"The world is your oyster, Adam. You are young, healthy, strong, and bright. You can do anything you want."

My mom was equally positive in her appraisal of my situation. "Adam, you are a bright young man with a bright future. All you need to do is apply yourself." But already I was beginning to revert to a selfish lifestyle. Rebelliousness ran rampant within me, as if I had graduated magna cum laude with a degree in "Being Difficult." What I wanted to do was the exact opposite of everything my dad or mom suggested. If Dad asked me to consider going back to school, my answer would be a terse, "No." If he suggested employment training of any type, my answer again would be, "No." Exasperated, but trying not to show it, my father would ask, "Well, what do you want to do with your life, Adam?"

My one-word reply was, "Work."

"Then goddamn it, get a job! You go get a job, not me get you a job. I already have a job for me. In fact, I have two jobs, and one of those jobs is you, and it pisses me off. It is wearing me out. You're wearing me out. Soon you'll be 23 years old. It's time you get off my tit."

I'm not sure why I resisted my parents' attempts to help

me get a start. Every young man wants to do his own thing, certainly; but at the same time, my progress in life had been slowed because of my drugging. I was smart enough to know I needed some guidance, but stupid enough not to take it when it was available. My long history of failure at jobs and school should have told me to shut up and listen up.

In the summer of 2000, one year after I graduated from high school, I enrolled at Triangle Tech Institute in Greensburg, Pennsylvania, for a two-year course in Heating Ventilation and Air Conditioning (HVAC). The school placed one hundred percent of its graduates at good paying jobs with promising career opportunities. Moreover, with credentials as a licensed HVAC technician, I could find a good job anywhere in the world.

My dad rented an apartment near the school and helped me furnish the place with dishes, silverware, coffee pot, radio, bedding, lamps and tables, and all other necessary household articles. An automobile was essential in order to commute among the various campuses in the area and to come home on weekends, should I desire. Therefore, Dad bought me an old beater.

I did come home on weekends, but not to visit my family. I came home for dope. Thirty-five days after classes began, I dropped out. Which I didn't care.

After Pap died in March 2001, I returned from Florida and started working at the Carpet Warehouse. Mostly, I loaded and off loaded carpet orders. I also cut carpet to size and performed inventory accounting. That job lasted approximately four months.

Off and on between "real" jobs, I delivered pizzas, and I worked at the Jiffy Quick carwash. Pizza delivery became mentally taxing, not because of the job requirements, but because I never worked for a manager who wasn't a prick, and it took too much psychic effort to hold myself back from going off on him.

One day I was summoned to work off-schedule because of a heavy demand for pizzas. Gold chain necklaces were taboo for the staff, but I was wearing mine when I reported for my first delivery. The manager climbed all over my frame just because I was wearing a gold chain. Apparently, he forgot that I was doing him a favor by reporting for work when I wasn't scheduled. So I snapped. I shot-putted my boxed pizza at him, telling him to "shove the pizza and the job up your ass." That ended my career as a pizza courier.

My tenure as a carwash professional was cut short when the Jiffy Quick manager, also a prick, discovered that the crew had figured out a way to skim some extra profits by bilking the customers. Super Washes cost $10, double the price of the regular soap and water job. When the customer requested a Super Wash, we took the $10 and, instead of pushing the button that sprayed Magic Wax and Miracle Rust Protection on the vehicle, we hit the regular button. This activated the chain which snagged a cog on the underside of the car and towed the dirty car through a line of mists and brushes and soaps and blowers. Presto! The car came out clean. Which was good enough. All the while, the unsuspecting customer stayed in his car smiling at us. It was pretty nice to take $5 off someone and watch him smile about it through a clean windshield. Anybody would think that's nice. I don't care who you are.

For two or three months in the Spring of 2002, I worked as a carpet installer. I earned $80 a day. Much of the work was in State College, Pennsylvania, an hour and thirty minutes drive east. Traveling back and forth every day was tiring. However, I liked installing carpets and quickly learned the trade. In no time I became expert at installing vinyl flooring as well as rugs.

One vinyl job at the University called for some tricky cutout patterns. Although I was the least experienced man on the job, I was the person who figured out the details from the drawings and scribed the floor to make the templates, with no instructions from my boss. There was no extra pay to come along with my talents, but I took a degree of satisfaction from doing good work.

I liked floor covering work and would have stayed, but one of my co-workers, the bosses' nephew, was using heroin, and it didn't take us long to find each other. As between the nephew and me, he kept his job and I was let go. The lesson learned: Don't work in a family run business – unless you want to get the shaft.

In the summer of 2002, I landed a job as an apprentice plumber. A family connection helped me get the job. Years ago, my boss, Bill, worked as a lead man in Pap's contracting business. Bill liked Pap, and now he needed a young man to help with his plumbing business. He thought why not teach me the trade. Pap had given Bill a job when Bill was a young man. Things had now come full circle with Bill giving me a job.

Pay was good at $12 an hour, and best of all, the Plumbers Union would cover the cost of my required schooling, which I could attend in the evenings just like Bill had done. After the apprenticeship, I would advance to registered Master Plumber.

My dad was thrilled that I had this opportunity. He said plumbers earn a lot more money than small town lawyers and they could be their own bosses. As hard as I tried, I couldn't last more than a day without getting high. My plumbing job ended after only five weeks.

The fact that I jumped the gun by leaving St. Jude's before I was ready and without a plan was starting to show. I heard my dad say many times if you fail to plan, you plan to fail. In my stubbornness, I thought this principle did not apply to me. Getting a job seemed to be all the aftercare that I needed. Inexperience led me to believe a job was plan enough.

In mid-January, 2004, I called a former employer, Tim Mikula, and asked if he was hiring. Tim was a former alcoholic and drug user who had discovered that life could be good without drugs and alcohol. After getting clean, Tim bought a basement waterproofing business. Quickly gross business volume rose to over a $1 million a year in sales. My dad was Tim's attorney. Through his relationship with Dad, Tim became aware of my problems with dope. Tim knew I had been at St. Jude's for the past seven months. Given my rehab, I hoped he would take a chance on me.

My personal history with Tim went back to the summer

of 2001. At that time, Tim arranged a meeting for me and my parents to try to persuade me to seek drug treatment. The formal term for trying to help someone who needs help and is unwilling to seek it on his own is "intervention," but I thought of it more as "intermeddling."

We met for lunch at the Holiday Inn. Tim told me he was speaking to me because he truly cared about me, and he was speaking from personal experience. That turned me off. At the time, the last thing I wanted to hear was a reformed alcoholic and doper preaching to me. Half the time while he was talking, I was looking away. Nevertheless, Tim ignored my rudeness and continued his pitch, while my mom and dad listened attentively.

"Adam, I'm 42 years old. I lived in the dark world of drugs and alcohol for too long. I'm not proud of that, but I can tell you it is not a life you want. I know how it feels to be high all the time. I also know how it feels to lie and cheat and steal. I know what it is like to destroy relationships, and your health, and your future. It was not too late for me to turn my life around, and I know, with help, you can do the same. What you're facing is powerful beyond comprehension. If you don't get help, you'll either go to jail, or you'll die. It's that simple."

Tim's attempt at intervention failed at the time, but I never forgot that he tried, and I truly believe it was from the heart. Knowing someone is on your side makes you feel good.

Given that Tim and I shared the horrible experience of drug addiction, when I asked Tim if I could get a job, he readily agreed to hire me. I would start working the following

Monday. Which was what I wanted.

The next several months were good for me. My brother Ben had returned from his overseas military duty and had re-enrolled at Indiana University of Pennsylvania. From time to time, I drove to see him at college and enjoy a taste of campus life. Insecurities from my history with drugs and the law, as well as my laborer's job, made me a misfit when I visited Ben and prevented me from hooking up with some cute coed. What could I say to attract a girl? – "Hi, I'm Adam, and I haul busted up concrete out of wet basements for a living." I'm sure I could have dated any college girl I wanted if I used that line.

My work at the waterproofing company was hard but honest, and for the first several weeks I saved a few bucks. Living at home cut my expenses to a minimum, so there was no reason for me to spend much of my paycheck. Like most young men, I wanted a new vehicle. Specifically, I was putting money aside to purchase a new Jeep Grand Cherokee.

My co-workers were wary of me at first, because I was the son of the company's lawyer. Those misgivings were allayed when they saw how many buckets of busted up basement floor I could haul to the truck in a day. Two at a time, all day long, I never let up. One or two of the guys would tell me, "Slow down, Adam. You're killing the job."

I loved hard physical work. For me it was a refuge, a place to hide within myself. The little interaction I had with my co-workers was incidental, such as bumming a smoke, or taking a lunch order, or asking for a hand. These guys were paycheck to paycheck guys, with pregnant wives or girlfriends, and sometimes both. I'm not saying I was better than them, but I came from a different social class. I know I was smarter than my co-workers, definitely.

A week or so after I started working, I looked up a couple of old girlfriends, more in my range. While at St. Jude's we weren't permitted to socialize with the female guests, which was understandable. Nevertheless, my young manhood had been deprived for too long. Unless I found a volunteer real quick, I was in danger of having the top of my head blow clean off.

Significant events in life need to be recognized. Wedding dates, graduations, birthdays, and the like are markers or milestones which punctuate a life. Dad thought my return from St. Jude's into the family fold was something that should be celebrated.

One year ago, in mid-March I had been kicked-out of my house for kicking-out the basement window and stealing Dad's 17-inch Sharp television and Bose wave radio. This March we would throw a homecoming party.

Why is it that every kid's grandma is the best cook? Of course, that is not true, except in my case. Grandma brought baked beans as only she knows how to prepare. She baked six pies, two each of apple, pumpkin, and coconut cream (for Uncle Ray). Aunt Jan showed up with a pineapple pastry dessert, the kind that causes you to pinch the serving knife between your fingers after each slice to clean off the good stuff, and then, when no one is looking, lick your fingers. Lisa and her mother and dad worked all day preparing old fashioned Hungarian pastries which they brought to the party.

There were jellos and fancy salads and cole slaw, chicken tenders and au gratin potatoes that I don't know who brought. For drinks, a crystal bowl with matching cups was filled to the brim with a cocktail of Hawaiian Punch, 7-Up, and orange sherbet.

To make the occasion special, Dad ordered a 40-pound roasted piglet with raisin stuffing from Froelich's Meat Market. Each celebrant would serve himself by hacking away at the pig with the nine-inch carving knife that lay beside it.

The feature dishes were not the roasted pig or Grandma's pies, they were Uncle Walt's appetizer dips. Gourmet cooking is one of Uncle Walt's hobbies. He showcased his talent at my party with four presentations; roasted eggplant, peanut sauce, baked artichokes, and Greek cucumber dip. My favorite was the peanut sauce which he made with hot shrimp paste, oyster sauce, natural peanut butter, ginger, lime, and brown sugar.

All Dad's office staff were present. My cousin Paul drove in from Virginia. Dad's Uncle Dean and Aunt Dorothy joined us. Fifty friends and family came to celebrate my success that afternoon. I got more than 250 hugs and handshakes from them.

There was hardly a person in attendance who I had not harmed in some respect while I was drugging. Some I had hurt deeply, like Grandma and Ben. In spite of that, everyone was cheering for me. What had I done to deserve such an outpouring of kindness? Really?

Dad set the roasted pig on the table and stuffed an apple in its mouth to finish the garnishing. The feast was about to begin. With only a gesture, people quieted and drew closer in the center room. After a pause, Dad spoke up, "Walter, will you lead us?"

"Oh, sure I will." Then Uncle Walt prayed, "Dear God, thank you for wrapping your arms around Adam and keeping him safe. Your love is a reminder to us all that we are not alone."

How good Grandma must have felt after the party as she stood at the kitchen sink washing the last of her pie plates, taking notice that not a single piece was left over. All of Uncle Walt's baked artichokes with peccarino romano cheese and garlic and lemon juice was scraped off the side of the serving dish. That night, those present at my homecoming rested better under the comforting belief that I was drug-free at last.

Of the four absolutes Calvin taught me: love, purity, honesty, and unselfishness, I stood in violation of all four – honesty being the most flagrant. Had I been honest with my guests, they would have known about my recent drug use. I tried to tell myself it was only crack, not heroin, and that I only picked up again one month ago, which was pretty good. My arguments were sound enough to convince anybody but me that I could quit again. I had learned to be happy without drugs. At the party, however, I felt isolated again. Only I knew the truth about my behaviors. Had I revealed to the others that I was using for five weeks, the occasion would have been a mockery. Everybody there saw my homecoming party as a cause for celebration. For me, it was a time for shame.

Car salesmen are about as good as any businessman at

keeping in touch with their clientele. Periodically they send out circulars, "Dear Valued Customer, We're running a special on all late model used cars. Please bring this notice with you when you visit us so you can take advantage of special pricing we are offering for you. Hope to see you soon." Drug dealers are good businessmen, just like car salesmen. If a dealer hasn't heard from his customer, he calls to find out what's wrong.

It was mid January, 2004, when Shaun started calling me on my cell.

"'Sup man, heard you was away. You back now. When I gonna hear from you, you know we have something going here."

I told Shaun I was working and had quit using the shit. No sense in him calling me.

"Yeah, well you say that now. But you be back. You working. I like to hear that. You call me. You know my number."

Twice a week for the next month I received a phone call from Shaun soliciting my business. I stayed away as long as I could, until one Friday after work when I got together with the guys from my crew for wings and beer at Murphy's Tavern. By 10:30 that night I was ready to pick up again. Shaun and I talked on the phone once more, except this time I placed the call.

Being off drugs for almost a year caused me to enjoy the first few puffs on the crack pipe more than usual. I planned to buy just two $20 rocks and figured I could stop at that, considering I had been without crack for almost a year, and I needed to save money for a nice Jeep. Shaun gave a doubting look when I laid down only $40. He took the $40 and smiled, knowing I was back on his list of preferred customers. By Sunday night, I had spent my $180 paycheck on crack. At $10 a drag, a laborer's wages won't last long.

Within a month after the homecoming party, my crack usage reached an all time high. Dad had become more trusting than ever. Stealing from his wallet was easier than before.

One day I came home from work unexpectedly, and as I entered the house I caught Dad replacing a loose fitting board on a false shelf in the stairway leading to the basement. He did not know I heard him.

After Dad left the house, I jiggled a few of the boards until I found the loose one. The hiding place was perfectly concealed. Even after the board was removed, there was nothing visible. Nevertheless, over the years I had repeatedly searched the entire house stick by stick looking for Dad's stash. It had to be here. Reaching my arm around the awkward corner and probing with my fingers, I found almost $10,000 in large denomination bills. Dad was putting a little cash aside to cover Ben's college expenses. I had better uses for the money.

C H A P T E R T W E L V E
Slipping

To this day, I do not know why I tried to hide my drug use from Dad. I believe if I had told him I picked up again, he would have understood. Make no mistake, he would have been angry as hell, but Dad would have gotten over that and offered help. I guess I didn't want to disappoint him again.

The only person I confessed to was my friend Michael. We talked on the telephone every day. Michael urged me to return to St. Jude's for a tune up. Something had not yet connected. A critical component was missing, and Michael wanted me to stop the skid before I slipped all the way to the bottom. Michael was tuned in to my struggles and was trying to forestall impending disaster. Which I appreciated.

There had been some changes at St. Jude's in the four months that passed since I left in late December, 2003. Michael was now an instructor, and Calvin had moved on. I think he was in Boston studying culinary arts. Becoming a chef was one of Calvin's dreams. I wished I could have talked to Pops, but, like I told him when I left St. Jude's, he had done all he could for me, and it was now my responsibility to apply what I learned.

Upon learning of my bad choices, I know what Calvin would have advised. He would have said, "Stay strong, Adam. Keep the faith, son." He would have told me to pray. Whenever I was confronted with a choice, Pops always told me to pray on it. I can still hear his baritone voice almost singing to me, "Pray not for what you want, Adam. Pray for what God will give you." To Calvin, the power of prayer could not be overstated, not that he was a religious fanatic, just that Calvin believed the spiritual element of a person works with the physical to complete the whole. He once told me, "Adam, if you're undecided about whether you should shit, pray on it. The answer will come."

One friend from Philadelphia who I met at St. Jude's wasn't so well-intentioned as Michael and Calvin. This fellow, Kevin, was a drop out. He lasted only two weeks before making the choice to return to drug use. Off and on Kevin and I talked by phone for several weeks, each phone call drawing me out a little more until I admitted to screwing up. He, too, had screwed up. Unlike Michael, Kevin wasn't trying to help me straighten out, he was working hard attacking my weakness.

"Adam, why don't you drive to Philly? We can have a great time."

Not very convincingly I answered, "I'm trying to quit that stuff, Kevin."

"Fuck it, Adam. Nobody beats addiction. You're fucked for life, and you know it. Might as well have fun while you can."

"Kevin, I work. I can't take off work."

"What about weekends? The drive can't be more than four or five hours. Come on Adam, let's have some fun."

Still resisting, I interjected a weak reason for not accepting Kevin's invitation to party with him. "If my dad found out, he would go ape shit on me."

"Fuck your dad. Be your own man, Adam. Live your life, don't let your dad try to live it for you. Good Philadelphia crack is twice as cheap as that shit you get out there in the woods. Come on, Adam, I have a glass stem pipe with your name on it. Can you bring $100? That is all you need to enjoy the whole weekend."

Paychecks were cut every Friday. Our crew finished a 65 foot job early Friday morning April 9, 2004, and it was too late to start a new job that afternoon. Better to wait until Monday so the homeowner doesn't have the house torn up over the weekend. Moreover, after busting hump all week with buckets, jack hammers, and wheel barrows loaded with concrete, our muscles were sore and our asses were dragging. I was psyched to have fun for a change.

With an early Friday quit and $200 in my pocket, I phoned Kevin and asked if I could visit on short notice. Without hesitation, Kevin answered, "Hell yes!"

The note on the counter at home read, "Dad, I went to visit a friend in Philadelphia for the weekend. I'll see you

Sunday night. Don't worry about me. I love ya. Adam"

Before leaving home, I grabbed an extra $200 from the secret vault, just to be certain I had enough money with me. Even when I wasn't drugging, I never seemed to have enough money, probably because I never learned self-discipline. Dad said I went through money like it grew on trees. Which was right.

I departed at 3:10 p.m., cruising east on the Pennsylvania Turnpike in the Ford Explorer, past the turn off to the family cottages in Bedford, through the tunnels, past Carlisle and across the Susquehanna River. At Valley Forge, I exited and followed Kevin's directions to the rendezvous point, a McDonald's restaurant situated exactly where he said it would be.

Two cigarettes later, Kevin showed up, looking paler than I remembered him, and less robust. I didn't know his age, but I guessed it to be 39 or 40. With dope, a person ages fast. Anybody would age fast if they did as much heavy shit as Kevin. I don't care who you are.

Houses in the surrounding neighborhood would sell for $150,000 to $200,000 back home, but probably twice that in suburban Philadelphia. Kevin's apartment was clean and nicely decorated. I figured he had a housekeeper or a good girlfriend who did all the work. From my experiences, dopers tend to be sloppy housekeepers. Kevin worked, but I don't know where. Every other weekend he had custody of his nine year old daughter. Perhaps that is why he kept such a clean apartment.

Our bender started when Kevin went shopping at his dealer's house and returned with $100 worth of crack. After we smoked that, he went back for more, and still more. By midnight Friday, we were totally blown away, as our drug orgy went into full swing. For the next three and a half days we never left the apartment except to resupply our crack. We puffed at such a frenzied pace that even hardcore users would have been impressed. Our stock of crack and money ran out early Monday afternoon. There went a week's paycheck. Not that I gave a rat's ass.

But wait! We were not finished. Down to the strip I went and traded away my special Seiko watch. My priceless watch – now worth only two small rocks.

The only thing I think about when I'm on a cocaine bender is cocaine. I don't think about food or medicine. The only food I ate from Friday evening through Monday was two bowls of cereal and some Ramen noodles. The Tegretol I brought along stayed in the travel case.

I called Mom to get more money, telling her I needed a few bucks for the trip home. She refused, saying she was tired of being played the fool while subsidizing my doping. I called my dad, and he threatened to "knock my goddamned head off" when he got hold of me.

At last, I called my boss, Tim Mikula. Tim had been in the gutters himself, and might show more understanding of my predicament. Instead of saying "No", Tim asked for a call-back number and told me to stand by, which I had no choice but to wait for a return call. Tim then called my dad.

"David, I just got a call from Adam. He wants me to wire money so he can come home. I told Adam I was going to call you."

"Do what you want, Tim. You're capable of deciding what to do. As far as I'm concerned, it's ok to let the little bastard die."

"David, I've been where Adam is. I know what he's going through."

"Do you know what everybody else has been going through? Do you think Adam is concerned about all the grief he has caused the family these past 12 years? Let the little bastard die, Tim. I don't give a goddamn what happens to him."

Lucky for me, Tim understood what was going on in my head better than Dad. An hour later, I took delivery of $50 from Western Union. Of the $50, $10 gassed the Explorer, and $40 purchased two more rocks, enough for a couple of bon voyage hits.

Twenty minutes into the return drive, Kevin called me on my cell phone to tell me he scrounged $50 dollars more and asked if I wanted to turn around and smoke it in crack. As he was asking the question, I was wheeling the Explorer around to go back.

These last two hits finally produced a brain overload. As I walked out Kevin's front path to the driveway, I felt light-headed and fuzzy. My body was telling me another drug induced seizure was on the way. As quick as I could, I found a soft spot in the yard off to the side, because I knew I would be flopping around when the seizure took hold. Soft earth would be kinder to my body. I dropped right onto mud just as the seizure grabbed me. While not conscious during the event itself, I recall a sensation in my brain as if it were shrinking and exploding in pulsating rhythms. I felt no physical pain, only those odd sensations.

I must have been on the ground at least 30-minutes before regaining consciousness because my red ski jacket was soaked through. The right side of my face was still imbedded in the mud, for I could feel my eyelid blinking against debris, and I was certain my right contact lens was scraped out and lost somewhere in the mud. Vision from the right eye was poor, and it felt as though the eyeball was scratched. That eye would not stop watering, and the more I rubbed it, the more it watered. A mouthful of dirt and stale spit ground against my teeth and choked me. When I stood up, my left shoulder dangled loosely by my side indicating my problem shoulder had again dislocated. Dr. Yardley's surgical repair 18 months ago was good enough to hold the shoulder through heavy weight training workouts at St. Jude's, but was no match for the forces imposed when the seizure struck. Intense pain from my shoulder produced a horrible taste in the back of my tongue.

Cold, broke, gagging, crippled, and blinded I limped to the Explorer and somehow pointed it west toward home. I called Dad and told him I had a seizure, hoping to pull off the road and wait for him to rescue me.

"I don't give a goddamn if you die on the road, Adam. You and your goddamn doping. You did this to yourself, now, goddamn it, live with it."

It wasn't physically possible for me to drive home. I was nearly passed out from pain, my body shivered uncontrollably under wet clothes, and my vision was blurred. On top of that, it was doubtful if there was enough fuel in the tank to climb to the top of Pleasantville Mountain. Getting stranded on the road would have been the end for me; maybe a fitting end to a tormented life that never reached its destination.

Each night when I was little, I used to say this prayer to my Guardian angel, "Angel of God, my Guardian dear, to whom God's love commits me here. Ever this night be at my side, to light and guard, to rule and guide." Perhaps God could send one of His angels to drive my car for the last 200 miles. If there truly were angels among us, I wanted one to come forth to steady my hand at the wheel, to clear my head, to sharpen my vision, to pour gas in my tank, and to take away my terrible pain. If it were not asking too much, I needed my angel to hang around and help me go on without the love and support of my earthly family, which I felt would be lost forever.

The hum of the tires and the rhythm of the road moved my car along with the rest of the Turnpike traffic. Once in a while, I would slip behind a big rig and draft it for 20 or 30 miles, never needing to steer or brake or accelerate.

At Bedford, I exited the Turnpike 34 miles short of my destination. Without money to pay the toll, I had to sign a form promising to pay within seven days or risk license suspension. Adding to my anxiety, my "Low Fuel" indicator had been flashing for 20-minutes. Now, if I could get over the

3,000 foot-high Pleasantville Mountain, probably I could coast the remaining 15 miles.

On fumes, the Explorer pulled into the driveway. I needed one more prayer answered, "Dear God, tell my dad to unlock the front door. Please ask him not to turn me away."

Angels held me up, one under each arm, as I walked from the car to the front door. The handle turned and the oak door swung open. Just as my legs gave out, Dad caught me. Tenderly he sat me on a chair and carefully removed my soggy, mud-encrusted, red ski jacket. He wrapped me in a warm blanket, picked me up in his arms, and carried my broken body to his car.

On the way to the hospital, my father's eyes welled with tears, but he held them in, and his voice remained steady. Dad said he would have to think about what I had done, but for the present, the issue was obtaining medical care. Which it was.

Two days later, after I got out of the hospital, we had our talk. My dad decided I would have to leave the house. He told me he would not "countenance a doper walking these floors any longer." As usual, Dad would pay for my medicines and other necessities so that I could live with dignity if I chose. Johnnie's Restaurant would honor my signature for meals, as much as I wanted. I should call for non-drug related emergencies, otherwise I was on my own.

In the past, Dad provided an apartment for me. This time he refused. My mom agreed to pay the rent, but she placed a $250 monthly cap. So what could I get for that but a shit hole?

A shit hole is exactly what I got. "Home" was a third-floor, vermin-infested hovel in the slum section of town. Ceiling lights were bare light globes hanging from a wire with a switch on the end where the globe screwed in. After a flush, the commode took twenty minutes to refill, which I didn't give two shits about. The hot water worked on the kitchen sink, but in the bathroom all you got out of the left side faucet was a trickle. The walls had been freshly painted thirty or forty years ago. The floor featured splinters and loose nails sticking up approximately one-quarter inch, just enough to tear open the bottom of my feet, or rip a toenail. The old-fashioned, high, poplar baseboard added a touch of class which was set off nicely by chipped dirty paint.

My mom helped me clean the place, but that place could only be adequately cleaned with a match. After two days of scouring and scrubbing, conditions upgraded from filthy to merely uninhabitable. The entrance door was on the second floor at the front of the stairs which ascended to the third floor nest. It locked from the inside only by wedging a length of pipe between the door and the third step. Old cast radiators threw off heat when the furnace ran, but it was April 17th and the cheap bastard landlord had already shut off the gas furnace.

Not long ago, I was living in a cozy modern home with two televisions, a refrigerator full of food, a nine-foot pool table, a weight room, an outdoor hot tub, and a gas grill. Not long ago the mother of all parties was thrown in that home celebrating my return. I found comfort knowing the people who loved me didn't see me hit bottom again.

X-rays of my shoulder revealed that a portion of the

humeral head had been sheared off at the time I went down with my last seizure. As a result, frequent dislocations would continue unless I underwent a second surgery to stabilize the shoulder joint. So severe was the damage that, for a while, it looked like my best option was a complete shoulder replacement. Although tricky, Dr. Yardley devised an alternative plan to tighten my shoulder with a series of pins and soft attachments. At my age, replacement was ill advised, and fusion of the shoulder was too limiting. We took a chance, and I had the operation.

My Dad was away when I had the surgery. So my mom drove me home from the hospital to my third floor apartment. For three days I laid up there on an old foam couch that I used as a bed. I was under instructions not to move my arm in any direction for at least two weeks, after which I would begin physical therapy.

Shaun started calling my cell phone, which Mom kept activated so she could stay in contact with me.

"'Sup man. Ain't heard from you in a while. What you doing?"

I told Shaun I had surgery on my shoulder and lost my job and got kicked out of the house, and therefore, I didn't have any money to buy dope.

"Hey, don't worry about that. You down now, but you get back up. You good for it. How bout I swing by and front you some, you know, you pay later. You cool with that? Hey where you living man? I come by now."

Of all the things in the world, crack was the thing I

needed least right then, but it was also the thing I wanted most. Shaun was instructed to meet me on the corner of Somerset Street and Franklin Street in fifteen minutes. He showed, and the deal went down. My name was scribed in his book for a $100 credit balance. This was the first time I was ever beholding to a drug dealer, and I didn't get good vibes. In the past, I was always able to "pay as you go." True, I did a lot of stealing to get the money, but when I bought dope, I paid cash. I was honorable.

Most of my buys were solo transactions, just me and the dealer. Danger lurked whenever a white kid sat alone in his car or stood outside in a public housing area until he was spotted by a dealer. The drug world knew what I was waiting for and that I had money with me. It became a race between the dealers, who zealously guarded their turf, and the punks with hand guns who tried to rob the users before the dealers were alerted that a customer was waiting.

During my drug days, guns were pulled on me four times by punks who spotted me before the dealer did. Two of these incidents ended in fights, with me winning one and getting pistol whipped in the other. On the other two occasions, after I was told to hand over my money or I would have "my fucking head blown off," I calmly smiled and said, "Go ahead. Blow my head off. You'll be doing me a favor." Both times, the chicken shit punks left cursing and threatening but didn't have the guts to back up the threat. Back then, I would have welcomed it if someone put a bullet in my head. Many times I thought of doing it myself.

While my shoulder was trying to get better, I continued to

get crack from Shaun. My bill was mounting, but I figured in time Dad would let me back in the house, and I could find payback money under the loose board.

Although I wasn't allowed to come home, Dad talked to me on the phone every day, and occasionally, he stopped to see me. On a bright Saturday, Dad and Lisa popped in after a motorcycle ride and brought groceries for me. Lisa tried to buy things that would not perish and could be eaten without much food preparation, because I still could not move my left shoulder.

Dad and I had a talk outside by the motorcycle. He said it was time for me to start thinking of a career. Acting on Dr. Dalton's advice, arrangements were made for me to undergo a battery of tests to be conducted by the Pennsylvania Office of Vocational Rehabilitation. Since I had nowhere to go but up, I heartily agreed.

Dad said everybody needs three things in order to live a fulfilled life; someone to love, something to do, and something to hope for. Finding someone to love might not be easy, but should be fun. I hoped I could become drug free, that one was easy. Having something to do was where the vocational rehab testing might come in to play. I wanted to take the tests as soon as possible. No point waiting for my shoulder to heal. I didn't need to use both arms to take a test that required only the use of my head. Tests were scheduled.

Only Mortals Can Be Heroes

CHAPTER THIRTEEN

Never Surrender

The mere presence of a man six feet five inches tall and 295 pounds was intimidating. Although he was soft spoken and polite, rumor around town had it that Shaun could be brutal. Some said he fled north from Baltimore to escape retaliation from family members of those who had tasted his ruthlessness. Extreme force was an occupational necessity in order to remain the Big Kahuna on the local drug scene.

It was May 9, 2004, three weeks after my shoulder surgery. Dr. Yardley had given me clearance to remove the shoulder sling in order to shower, but that was it. He wanted at least another month for the body to heal before starting physical rehabilitation. Although not normally compliant with medical instructions, this time I did what I was told and kept my left arm still. In my filthy apartment, I laid on the foam sofa and watched the one snowy channel my television could receive without a cable connection. Aside from a dose of ringworm the size of a quarter on the back of my right chicken wing, I was hanging tough.

My cell phone went off, " 'Sup man. How you doing? I need to talk to you." Shaun again! All I could think about was the $450 that I owed him. It made no difference to Shaun that I had been unable to leave my apartment until just a few days ago. Payment was overdue.

"Hey, man, I know you want your money, but I need another day or two, that should be enough time."

"No, that's cool, don't worry about paying me now. I want to talk to you. I have something you might like to hear. You stop by and see me tonight, cool?"

"Yeah, ok. I'll be down."

Shaun's business was run out of a first-floor apartment in one of the public housing projects in Johnstown. The apartment was in his name, but he paid no rent. Due to a congenital heart irregularity, Shaun was put on Social Security Disability and drew a monthly paycheck from the federal government, plus a bundle of other entitlements such as public housing eligibility, food stamps, medical assistance, education assistance, and job training. Be assured, Shaun had no interest in following through with either education or job training. As for education, Shaun had a master's degree in "Beating the System." For work, Shaun was an entrepreneur par excellence, directing a business which generated a million dollars plus in annual non-reportable income.

Tonight would not be the first time I drove to Shaun's apartment, but these circumstances were different from before. Something in the tone of Shaun's soft voice alerted an instinct in me to be on the lookout for any signs of the unusual. On all previous dealings I had at least $40 with me for crack. Sometimes Shaun would "front" me some extra crack, with the cost tacked on my next bill. I couldn't figure out why Shaun wanted to see me tonight, knowing I was broke. Oh, what the hell, there was nothing good on the tube at 8 p.m., and I didn't have any other plans. So I drove to Shaun's place.

As I approached, the door opened without my knocking. Crack dealers always have muscle around them. Shaun's muscle doubled as doormen. He kept two guys near him at all times, not as big as Shaun, but built like strong safeties. I recognized the faces on these two characters from being at Shaun's before, but I never did learn their names. In fact, I never heard either of them utter a word. I dubbed these cretins, "Einstein and Edison."

Our usual course of dealing was for me to pass through security, walk into the kitchen, and find Shaun sitting at the table. I would tell him how much money I had, and he would signal Einstein or Edison. One would leave the room for a few minutes and then return with the right amount of dope. As I walked into the kitchen this time, Shaun was standing.

"Adam, you owe me $650. When you gonna pay it?"

"I told you I needed a day or two to get the money. I just got over surgery, and my arm is still in a sling as you can see. Anyway, I only owe you $450."

Still soft spoken and smiling, Shaun said, "My books say $650. You know, interest. Can you pay today?"

Of course I could not pay. Usually I am quite glib and

able to talk my way around any situation. The atmosphere at that time didn't lend itself to smooth talking.

"Look. How bout you do a little selling for me to work off the debt. That way we both win. That is really why I called you down here."

I thought, "Oh, so that's the deal. Shaun wants me to sell for him."

Relapse is bad enough; becoming a dope dealer is going past the point of no return, and I would not consent to the latter. "I don't think so. I'll get you paid quick, ok?"

Still smiling, Shaun said he understood that I wasn't interested in working for him and that I did not have the $650 with me. I nodded agreement to Shaun's summary of the situation.

"All right, Adam, you might as well leave. We done talking."

Relieved, I headed toward the front door. My walk was rudely interrupted when I felt a hard chop to the base of my skull which knocked me head first onto the floor. I got to my knees where my face presented an even more inviting target. Quickly, I was flattened again with a boot to my face. This time I stayed down and tried to cover up. My efforts to protect myself were hampered because my left arm was immobilized by the recent surgery and by the sling which kept the arm attached to my side with velcro. As a result, half my head and face remained exposed. Einstein and Edison kicked and hammered me non-stop for over a minute. They quit only after I lost consciousness.

It must have been five or six hours before I came to my senses. All that time I laid on the sidewalk in front of Shaun's apartment in Building 14. Not one Good Samaritan offered assistance. With every heartbeat I could hear blood pulsing past my left ear, as if it were equipped with a built-in stethoscope. Using my right arm, I felt around the contour of my face and could tell it was so severely swollen that it took on an elliptical shape. Breathing through my nose was labored, and breathing through my mouth irritated the open wounds on my tongue. My legs and back seemed undamaged. Apparently most of the kicks landed on my head. A few must have reached my left shoulder because it felt as though someone was trying to cut it off with a rusty crosscut saw.

Realizing I could not lay on the sidewalk all night, I got to my feet and searched for the Explorer. It was gone. My feet would have to take me to safety.

The distance between Shaun's place and my dad's home was seven miles, four miles beyond my shit hole apartment, but in the same direction. If I walked to my apartment where I would be alone, I might die for want of medical care. If I walked the additional four miles home, I might die on the way. Faced with these choices, I decided to risk the longer walk to Dad's house.

Route 56 follows the Conemaugh River east through town, then begins its ascent to the higher ground where Dad's house is located. In the early morning hours there was no danger from traffic, so the path that offered the best chance of making it to Dad's was along the right hand berm of the four lane expressway. There I plodded, step after step.

Twelve years of drugging passed in review during my long march home. With all the beatings, injections, guns to my head, overdoses, needles, seizures, and surgeries, how could I still be alive? As I tramped the roadside gravel, I had no ready answer to this question. Every step sapped strength from my battered body. I began to comprehend the temporary nature of life and the finality of death. Death had tried to take me on several occasions, but thus far had failed. Would this be the night death triumphed? If so, bring it on!

I looked at dying from the other side of the hotcake. Could it be that God decided it wasn't time to come for me? Not long ago, He sent angels to care for me. I was spared. Could it be that God wasn't finished with me? Was He allotting more time to carry out His plan? Who can know?

Four miles into the trek, exhaustion set in and I had to sit on a guardrail, then directly on the ground, and finally I laid on my back looking up. Black enveloped my whole world at that moment, not even a twinkle of light came from the heavens. Blood was wooshing inside my left ear, sounding like a small stream was flowing within my head. My tongue was swollen to such a degree that it obstructed air passage down my windpipe into my lungs. My face, especially on the left side, was stretched so tight that it was ready to split at any moment, like a head of flat Dutch cabbage after a soaking rain.

Fifteen minutes of rest allowed me to regain some strength. There was no choice but to walk-on in the darkness. Using my good right arm, I leveraged myself onto my feet and continued the homeward march.

At 6:20 in the morning, I got to the house. The first thing

I did was check the garage to see if Dad's car was there. It was. Upon entering, I found the house to be quiet. I wasn't sure how to tell Dad what happened to me, but I figured the answer would come out soon enough. Too afraid to call out, I sat at the kitchen table and waited for Dad to find me.

Ten minutes later, Dad came down the stairs to grind his coffee. He could see my mangled head and raccoon eyes. Without saying a word, Dad took hold of my good arm and led me to the mirror in the foyer.

"Take a look, Adam. See what drugs do!" After a pause and some head shaking, Dad added, "Well, I guess we have no choice, do we. Get in the car."

Central Hospital has a drive up ramp for emergency vehicles, but Dad did not pull there. He stopped in front of the building on Main Street and said to me, "Here is where you get out, Adam. You had enough strength to walk home, you will have enough to get yourself admitted."

I opened the door and stumbled on the curb. Dad drove away leaving me standing in front of the hospital.

For the most part, pain was minimal. If it weren't for the severe headaches, I probably would have walked away when Dad dumped me at the front entrance to Central Hospital. I was always able to cope with pain, even extraordinary pain, but the headaches told me my condition was worse than mere pain and needed medical attention. Therefore, I followed the signs which guided me through the hospital maze to the Emergency Room.

My head had been bashed out of symmetry and took on

the form of a crooknecked squash. One look at its shape and size provided reason enough for the Emergency Room team to order a CT scan. Emergency protocol required a look at the inside. Good thing they did, for I had suffered a basilar skull fracture, a left temporal contusion, a subarachnoid bleed, and a broken nose. On top of this, one lady doctor also said I had a hemotympanum on the left. I took this to mean something was wrong with my left ear, and that is why I could hear the blood rushing past.

Following the CT scan, I was wheeled to the Intensive Care Unit for monitoring. To my surprise and delight, my body was not punctured with needles, nor was my throat clogged with a plastic tube. All my lower orifices were left undisturbed. What a relief! A clip was snapped over my index finger and various wires were glued to different parts of my chest and head. A green screen oscillated overhead behind my bed, and a soft "beep" could be heard every time the white line jumped a little. Nurses told me I would be monitored for three days.

By all indications, after the first critical twelve hours passed, my body would recover on its own from the physical injuries I suffered in the beating. Youth must be served. What really distressed me throughout my hospital stay was the loneliness. Nobody was on my side anymore, not even my father. On the afternoon of my first day in Intensive Care, my dad marched past security directly into the Unit and put his finger in my face. Actually the tip of his finger touched the tip of my nose. He did all the talking, and left no doubt I was on my own. In my head I couldn't blame him for abandoning me, but in my heart I hoped he would not disown me quite yet.

Through two more days of temperature taking and bedside urinals, I lay contemplating my plight.

Because of my depression, Dr. Fred ordered a psychiatric consult. Immediately prior to discharge, I was interviewed by a psych nurse.

Her note read:

> *". . . Patient apparently not able to return to father's home. States has nowhere to go- aware of Salvation Army but states will not go back there. Not sure of his plans, states he will live on the streets again, has done this in the past in the winter, summer will be "no big deal." Refuses to consider any treatment options locally. Wants to return to New York where he had treatment in past (recently returned) but has no $ to travel, parents paid for treatment in NY & according to Pt does not plan to pay again. Pt. was not receptive to shelter housing options. Is hopeless and helpless. Refuses any outpatient care. Pt. aware SS avail if he needs assist making some inquiries before d/c."*

Three days after admission, I sat signing discharge papers, feeling about as despondent as I could ever remember. My car was stolen and probably wrecked. My shoulder was in a sling. My mouth was too sore to eat. My face was disfigured. My pockets were empty, and my family had banished me. Under these circumstances, anyone would feel despondent. I don't care who you are.

I took two steps down the hospital corridor on my way toward the exit when I heard a familiar voice calling, "Get your chin off your chest, Adam. Show some pride. Stand tall and pull your shoulders back. Let's get rid of that hang-dog look." It was my dad! Somehow he found out when I would be discharged, and he came to pick me up.

From the hospital we drove to the Phoenix Tavern, which features good home style cooking. My dad doesn't like to eat at chain restaurants. He believes life is too short for fast food. In any event, eating was secondary to the reason we stopped at the Phoenix. We were there to talk. Which was a good idea.

Sitting opposite me and leaning a little forward, Dad calmly explained his analysis of the situation. While to some my relapse might be viewed as failure, to us it should be seen as a learning experience. We should try to discover why I failed, and fix it so I would not fail again. Holy cow! If I had learned even a tidbit from each of my failures, imagine how smart I would be now.

All the threats of abandonment and writing me out of his life were caused by frustration and disappointment, and, though real at the time, abandonment would almost certainly result in tragedy as the final outcome. Abandonment would be the same as giving up, or surrendering. On that issue, Dad said he stood with Winston Churchill, saying we should "Never Surrender!" Our objective was to defeat drug addiction. Both of us needed to use our heads and make the best decisions, not based on emotion, but rather, based on our best thinking.

When my turn came to talk, I told Dad that I already knew why I failed. Leaving St. Jude's without an intention to practice what I learned is why I relapsed. The solution was to return to St. Jude's with a brighter attitude, and specifically, to work on my after care plan.

Meanwhile, the cost of the six-week program had risen to $9,050. After the money my parents had already shelled out for me, there was no way I was asking them for more. I told Dad I had reached the low point in my life. Nothing was going my way.

"Adam, do you remember hearing the story of Mr. Penny's Pet Shop when you were just a little boy?"

"I might recall, kinda." I said.

Then Dad told me the story again, just the way he learned it from Pap. "Mr. Penny owned a pet shop, and in that shop he had three animals who were best friends. There was a doggie, a kitty, and a birdie. One day a man came into Mr. Penny's Pet Shop and bought the birdie. All the animals were sad that the birdie would be leaving, but before he left, the birdie said to his friends, 'Don't worry. Everything will be all right in the end.'

Although sad that their friend had gone, the doggie and kitty still had each other. Soon a woman came into Mr. Penny's Pet Shop and purchased the doggie. This caused the doggie and the kitty to be sad because they would be separated, but the kitty told the doggie not to cry, that maybe he would be lucky and go to a good home. As he was leaving, the doggie said to the kitty, 'Don't worry. Everything will be all right in the end.'

The kitty tried to be brave because she was all alone, but no matter how hard she tried, the kitty felt sad. Later that afternoon a little girl came into Mr. Penny's Pet Shop and bought the kitty.

That night there was a birthday party for Johnny, a seven-year-old boy. For a birthday present, his father gave the boy the birdie that he bought at Mr. Penny's Pet Shop. His mother gave Johnny the doggie, and his sister gave him the kitty. All three friends had been reunited in a good home! So, you see, everything turned out all right in the end."

Certainly life is more than fairy tales and children's stories, but they are part of life and real to me. Truth in any form is still truth. That night I slept with a serenity I had never before known. As if a spell were broken, the distant drums were silenced, gone from the back of my head, not even an echo calling.

For the next two days, I reveled in my nice home and slumbered peacefully in my clean bed, still uncertain about my future, but beginning to think I might have one. On the third day, city police called Dad and reported they had found the stolen Explorer, and it was in good shape. There was no need to write a formal report, since the vehicle was not involved in any type of incident. With no written report, there would be no newspaper account of the auto theft. Thank God! The family was being spared a public scandal.

Good things continued to happen when Dad said he and

my mom had agreed to give me another shot at St. Jude's. Even more encouraging, Dad had already sent a deposit to hold a bed. Since I was on probation in Pennsylvania, I couldn't just leave without court permission, but Dad said getting the green light was little more than a legal formality.

On May 21, 2004, almost a year to the day from my first trip to St. Jude's, I jumped in a rental car to go back. This time, failure never crossed my mind.

CHAPTER   FOURTEEN

Dreams

Within a week of my return to St. Jude's, I was adopted again. This time by a family I had never met. My adopting family came from Georgia, Colorado, Massachusetts, South Carolina, Rhode Island, Oregon, the Bahamas, Greece – everywhere. Each of my new brothers and sisters was at various stages of the treatment plan, hoping he or she could learn to be happy without alcohol or drugs. We all wanted to be responsible individuals, to make our families at home proud of us. We wanted someone to love. We wanted our dreams to come true once in a while.

The first weekend back, in late May 2004, twelve guests from the Wells home joined with twenty-four others from the St. Jude's mother house in Hagaman for a picnic on the shores of Lake Sacandaga. Cool breezes blew across the big water and freshened our lungs and our spirits as we tossed horseshoes, played volleyball, fished, and sat around the fire enjoying each other's companionship. At dark, play ended and all of us returned home for another week of self-examination and learning.

Weeks turned into months, and after my formal hitch was up, I became a "step and fetch it" who performed odd jobs such as running errands, picking up guests and driving them to the Albany airport, cleaning floors and bathrooms, and doing general maintenance work. Helping others, even in this menial manner, was satisfying to me, not that I liked doing mindless tasks, but because I stood on the giving end for a change. Moreover, being useful around the house fueled my hopes of earning an instructor position on staff.

From time to time, Calvin called me from Boston where he was studying culinary arts. Calvin always called in the evenings after the group session, when he knew I would be present. There were two payphones at the Retreat House for the convenience of the guests. When Calvin called for me, whoever answered would yell, "Phone call for Adam!"

As soon as I said, "Hello," the laughter began. Then I thought, "Oh shit, here it comes." Sure enough Calvin was on the other end checking to see how I was doing. He started our conversations the same way every time.

"You know who this is, son? This is your Pops." Calvin would laugh some more, then he would get serious. "You didn't forget what I taught you, son. Don't you ever forget how beautiful life can be. We came a long way together, you and me. Remember especially, if you're ever in doubt about what to do, pray on it. The answer will come. Promise me you won't forget."

Of course, I promised never to forget, and I told Calvin I was always here for him, if he ever needed me. After all, he was my Pops.

On Sunday, November 14, 2004, two weeks after my last conversation with Calvin, I received bad news. Pops had died from a heroin overdose. In the past, no other death hit me so hard. Life had meaning to me now.

I kept my promise to Calvin and didn't forget to pray. As Calvin had earlier instructed, I prayed not for what I wanted, but rather for what God might give. What I had wanted was for Calvin to live a long life in peace and happiness. What God would now give, I did not know.

On Sunday I called my dad and told him the sad news. We talked it out and reached some conclusions. Even though we couldn't bring Calvin back, I could draw on the spirit of Calvin's life to bolster my resolve to remain drug free forever. I would honor Calvin by living my life full, like he wanted.

Maybe Pops would be alive today if he had remained true to the precepts he had been taught. Instead, Calvin got involved with a female guest and was promptly dismissed from St. Jude's. Was this a moment of selfishness and dishonesty that cost Calvin his best chance of enjoying a normal and happy life, or was Calvin simply searching for someone to love – but in the wrong place and under the wrong circumstances. In life, human frailty sometimes defies reason.

After Calvin's indiscretion came the drugs, then the overdose. How quickly we forget that death is only one mistake away. Like the rest of us, Calvin had his weaknesses. Like the rest of us, Calvin took a chance at life. Unfortunately, for him life was too overwhelming outside of a controlled environment. Still, he took his humanity, strengths and weaknesses alike, and risked death in the hope of grabbing for the happiness that awaits us all. Now I understood what Uncle Walt meant when he sent that letter to me in jail. Only mortals can be heroes because only mortals risk death. The all-powerful gods never die. Was Calvin a hero? I don't know. He was to me.

Word must have spread to Grandma that I was feeling blue because of Calvin's death. Which I was. Hoping to cheer me, one week later Grandma mailed my favorite chocolate cake with cream cheese icing. For a moment, I became selfish again, and cut a big piece out of the corner for me. The rest went on the dining room table for my St. Jude's family, where it disappeared within minutes.

On December 17, 2004, my Guardian Angel whispered in my ear, "Adam, it is time for you to go home."

Leaving the comfort and safety of St. Jude's was scary, but weighing against that fear was the excitement of participating in life. It struck me as I drove away that altogether I had spent 16-months getting ready for this very moment. Whether I was adequately prepared, only time would tell.

Waiting on God to reveal His plan for me might take too long. I thought I would help Him out a little and do some planning for myself. As it stands, I plan to go to college and major in Human Services, with the hope of becoming a counselor. According to the tests I took in April at the Vocational Rehabilitation Center in Pennsylvania, I have the ability and the aptitude for this type of career.

As I see it, I am not on the road to recovery. I am on the

road to discovery. As I discover the new route, I will never forget the old way. Strewn along the old path are ruined relationships, lost opportunities, thousands of dollars stolen, money spent on treatment, damage done to my body, and near-death experiences. I hope it is not too late for me to discover how it feels to live with pride and respect. My family will stick with me until I catch up on lessons I should have learned long ago. With their help, perhaps I can become a son, a brother, a cousin, a nephew – who knows? Maybe even a hero. But whatever type of person I turn out to be, it has to be better than the person I was. I already am.

Embracing my past and accepting all of the bad things I did is part of the plan God has for me. Without experiencing the darker side of life, I would not be able to understand the pain of those who are presently overwhelmed by drugs or alcohol. If I can, I will help them. Whether my help takes the form of active counseling or is merely passive support, I will give everything I have, unselfishly, honestly, purely, and lovingly, just like Calvin taught me.

It is clear that I am God's special child. The circumstances of my birth no longer cause distress. Being adopted makes me special. My birth mother loved me enough to let me be born. The alternative was abortion. To mother, whoever you may be, I promise to honor you, by living my life as best as I can.

Discovering life includes discovering one's self. In my case, I have discovered that my body can be strong and fit. I feel energized and vigorous. Once again, I can be "The Little Engine That Could" and lead my group to the summit, like I did when we climbed the Adirondacks in six inches of early winter snow.

Twelve years of hiding my true feelings and vulnerabilities is bad, but not as bad as hiding from my feelings and vulnerabilities. The former is telling a lie to those who wanted to love me. The latter is telling a lie to myself. Strong in body, strong in spirit, I no longer need to hide from anything.

With dreams come hope, and I learned to dream. Some day there will be a girl who will love me, and whom I will love in return. Some day, just maybe, our children will help us decorate a Christmas tree, their young hearts bubbling with joy and spirit. Some day I will wrap my arms around my family so they will know they are not alone.

I cannot know the end of my life, but I do believe I have come to the beginning – the beginning of a real life. The story of Mr. Penny's Pet Shop is my story. I can hear the doggie, the kitty, and the birdie telling me, "Don't worry, Adam. Everything will be all right in the end." Which it is. Anybody would have to agree. I don't care who you are.

The View From the Window

David Weaver's building is a beautiful remodeling of one of those late 1800, early 1900 commercial properties we are so accustomed to seeing in the downtowns of America. One of the most appealing aspects of the remodeling was the installation of a floor-to-ceiling, smoked glass window wall serving as an end to the second floor and offering a wonderful view of Main Street below.

I was fortunate to occupy an office in the building and spent many happy hours with my landlord and friend discussing the passing scene on the busy street below. Politics, families, legal proceedings, sports, rumors, jokes, all became grist for the discussion mill. I have many fond memories of discussions ranging from trivial to important topics while we sat gazing out of that window.

The window holds many other memories as well. It was the perfect bad weather vantage point to watch parades. In fact, that is where I first met David's sons, Ben and Adam. They, along with my two daughters and other children, would run in and out of the building, upstairs and down, alternating between catching candy thrown from the floats and eating pizza and Mexican food from a spread laid out on the law library table.

I remember one Halloween parade, David's father Clair, then in his 80s, led the parade dressed as Uncle Sam in a beautiful costume made by his wife. Not only did Mr. Weaver walk the entire parade route but he crossed the street from curb to curb to personally greet the onlookers, much to the delight of the crowd and grandsons Adam and Ben. At the other end of the parade was the boys' father riding a spirited, high stepping horse with David dressed in full western attire. I can still remember the pride in the faces of the boys as they yelled, "There's Dad!" Times were good!

But nothing stays the same forever. The economy in the city and the surrounding areas declined rapidly. And you could see it from the window. The decreased foot traffic and the increasingly impoverished appearance of those who passed by the window. David saw it too but chose to maintain his law practice in the downtown, remaining faithful to the city that had been home to his family for generations. Remaining steadfastly loyal to those for whom he cares deeply, his bravery and willingness to take a risk and his fearlessness are high on the list of David's endearing character traits.

By the time I was forced to commute long distances for work, the view from the window of Main Street showed its worst decline as drug trafficking came to predominate. Between client appointments, I watched drug dealers operate their spots from a cross-street that faced David's building.

I remember David calling me one Sunday afternoon when Adam had become increasingly unruly and oppositional. I warned him of the increased likelihood of drug use that often accompanies this pattern of behavior. This book chronicles the efforts made to battle Adam's use of substances, much of it without positive consequence. Adam abused substances, ultimately becoming addicted, polysubstance dependent to be technical.

For many years I worked with teens adjudicated delinquent. My career path also led to employment in the Commonwealth of Pennsylvania, Department of Corrections where I worked in prison directly with inmates. The adult inmates always were curious about and interested in discussing my work with juveniles. Many adult inmates related how timely intervention in their teenage years might well have kept them from graduation to adult incarceration.

One inmate in particular likened the last opportunity to help a teen to looking out of a window while being seated in a room. A teen enters your view from the window and then passes from your line of sight. The inmate equated these views as 11-12 to 16-17. This age range represented the period when you have some chance of impacting positively on the youth. Always the inmates asked that I convey this information to the parents of delinquent youth and I have done so and did so with David.

Many therapists advise parents with addicted children who have proven recalcitrant to treatment to save themselves, to not let the addicted, now young adult, destroy their lives, especially if the child has passed by the window. I passed this information on to David as well.

I continue to maintain an office in David's building. Although I am rarely there anymore, I always look at the window as though I expect to see Adam enter and pass from my view followed by a doggedly determined David guided only by his loyal, loving, caring, and brave inner-self, not caring about age limits, the odds, saving self, or other barriers, but simply David once again brooking no obstacles on his way to his goal.

David, I know that in the past we have said this to each other with the utmost sincerity, but again, you really and truly are one of my heroes. I believe that in time and with continued abstinence, Adam will come to view you as his hero as well.

Raymond F. Dalton, Jr.
Psychologist